STOPS ALONG
THE ROYAL ROAD

To: SANDY
An O.T.s friend
and gentleman

E——Bey

2018

STOPS ALONG THE ROYAL ROAD

Adventures from a Lifetime of Travel

By Ernest Beyl

GRIZZLY PEAK PRESS
350 Berkeley Park Blvd. Kensington, CA 94707

For information contact:
Grizzly Peak Press
350 Berkeley Park Boulevard
Kensington, CA 94707
grizzlypeakpress.com

Stops Along the Royal Road
is published by Daniel N. David
and is distributed by Grizzly Peak Press.

Cover: The author in a bar at the Oceano Hotel in Puerto Vallarta.
Photo: From the collection of Ernest Beyl

Design, layout and typesetting by
Sara B. Brownell • sarabbrownell.com

ISBN Number: 978-0-9988310-2-2
Library of Congress Number: 2017964205

Printed in the United States of America

Ah, but I was so much older then
I'm younger than that now

My Back Pages
Bob Dylan

We shall not cease from exploration
And the end of all our exploring
Will be to arrive where we started
And know the place for the first time.

Four Quartets
T.S. Eliot

A Few Comments on *Stops Along the Royal Road*

"Ernest Beyl has created a travel journal for the quixotic journeyman and adventurer poet, seamlessly weaving his own explorations with inspirations derived from some of the world's most compelling authors, historians, journalists and adventurers. From his time as a U.S. publicist for globe-trotting heavy-hitters such as Cathay Pacific Airways and Hong Kong & Shanghai Hotels to his adventures reporting throughout Asia and visit to his father's homeland in Strasbourg, Beyl's book is peppered with memorable characters and life musings.

On every page, I am reminded of the travels to be taken, the relationships to be forged, and the life to be lived, should one seek it out. Beyl's anecdotes of chance, culinary curiosities and even catastrophe will make you want to dust off that rucksack languishing in the closet, throw in a blank journal and hit the road. Filling the journal's pages will only be half the adventure…

Travel has always been one of the great joys of my life, not just to escape from the daily grind of politics but also to seek out new perspectives and insights. If I'm not traveling to new parts of the globe or returning to beloved communities, the next best thing is living those experiences vicariously through the pages of a well-written book. A good travel yarn immerses one in the sights, sounds and smells of another place and time—and the unique human experiences that bend the course of history and shape our future decisions."

–Aaron Peskin, District Three, Board of Supervisors, San Francisco

"The champion flaneur of North Beach now shares his rich memories of wanderings beyond San Francisco. If there were a bohemian café at the North Pole, Ernie Beyl would surely find a polar bear on the premises to join him in paw-shakes and conversation. He evokes resorts far and dear—for example, the Brasserie Lipp at St.-Germain-des-Pres in Paris. But Ernie, did you enjoy sitting near the starlets with the yapping poochlets, feeding them with morsels of the *cervelas* (an un-American hot dog) on their laps?"

–Herbert Gold, author of *When a Psychopath Falls in Love*
and *Not Dead Yet*

"My earliest excursions with Ernie Beyl took place around 1966 at the Monterey Jazz Festival. I was an up-and-coming young musician with Memphis roots and he was an 'established' PR man who knew everything about San Francisco and beyond. From Sam's Grill to a dimly lit dive in Chinatown where our private dining cubicle was adorned with an antiquated brass buzzer to alert the waiter of our culinary desires. After lunch we would stroll leisurely and duck into obscure alleys laden with Barbary Coast ghosts. Traveling with Ernie is like discovering the world when it was an open oyster. With delight and wonder he spins his web of intrigue, discovery and history. Each vignette in this book rewards us with a rare pearl. Collectively he has created a gem of a travelogue."

–Charles Lloyd, international concert and recording artist and
National Endowment for the Arts Jazz Master

TABLE OF CONTENTS

Foreword xiii

Introduction xvii

CHAPTER 1: Mister Emmrich's Frousy Fanny 1

CHAPTER 2: Shanghai 1947 8

CHAPTER 3: Shanghai 1995 15

CHAPTER 4: A Picnic with Emperor Zhu Houcong in the Valley of the Ming Tombs 17

CHAPTER 5: Dutch Colonialism gave Us Rijsttafel 20

CHAPTER 6: The Years Haven't Been Kind to Don Francisco Pizarro 23

CHAPTER 7: Peru's Porno Pottery 25

CHAPTER 8: MacArthur's Car 28

CHAPTER 9: Visiting Emperor Hirohito 32

CHAPTER 10: Oddities and Oddments 35

CHAPTER 11: Inca Ghosts at Machu Picchu 38

CHAPTER 12: Discovering Hong Kong 43

CHAPTER 13: Alsace Lorraine: It's all in the Family 53

CHAPTER 14: Bung Sukarno's Man 57

CHAPTER 15: Bali: The Morning of the World 60

CHAPTER 16: Lei Yue Mun.. 63

CHAPTER 17: Whatever Happened to Jim Thompson?..................... 68

CHAPTER 18: Mongkok and the Snake Shop 70

CHAPTER 19: Port Out, Starboard Home with the P&O: Fiji to San Francisco aboard S.S. Himalaya 73

CHAPTER 20: Traveling and the Life of a Serious Eater.................... 77

CHAPTER 21: Dining with the Doctor in Singapore......................... 83

CHAPTER 22: Antonio's Embarrassment: Matador Ordonez in Mexico 85

CHAPTER 23: Angel Falls.. 89

CHAPTER 24: I Have Laid Aside Business and Gone A' Fishing....... 92

CHAPTER 25: It Happened in Sun Valley.......................... 94

CHAPTER 26: Taylor "Beartracks" Williams 96

CHAPTER 27: Fishing with Hemingway's Fly Rod........................... 98

CHAPTER 28: Papa Hemingway and Gary Cooper 100

CHAPTER 29: Blue Damsels and Cold Vodka.................................. 103

CHAPTER 30: Bugis Street Revisited 106

CHAPTER 31: The Nonya Food of the Strait of Malacca.................. 107

CHAPTER 32: The Old-Time Hollywood Glam Restaurants............. 110

CHAPTER 33: Mediterranean Miscellany 115

CHAPTER 34: At My Table.. 119

CHAPTER 35: Jeff Encounters Hong Kong........................... 124

CHAPTER 36: Shopping is Therapy Raised to the Tenth Power.......128

CHAPTER 37: The Broth of Chinese History....................................131

CHAPTER 38: Santiago de Compostela 134

CHAPTER 39: Liz and Dick at Gringo Gulch 138

CHAPTER 40: Rock 'n' Roll and the Art of Fly Fishing 143

Acknowledgments, Sources and Inspirations...151

About the Author...155

Index...157

FOREWORD

If there was ever a guy who could write an enjoyable, true book about travel and cultural experiences it's my Dad, Ernie Beyl. I remember when I was a kid, he took me crawdad fishing. We drove north from San Francisco across the Golden Gate Bridge up to Mount Tamalpais. We stopped at a small grocery store along the way and bought some bacon and some kite string. When we got farther up the mountain we parked along the edge of the road and hiked down to a small stream. The water was smooth and clear and we could see the rocks and boulders studding the bottom. We could see fingerling trout finning in the easy current, and looking closely we could see reddish crawdads hiding in the rock crevices. We wrapped pieces of bacon around small pebbles that we picked up along the edge of the water and tied that to a length of the kite string. We threw it out into the water somewhat in front of a crawdad and waited. When a crawdad emerged from hiding and grabbed the rig with its claws and began eating the bacon, we slowly brought it in, hand-over-hand, like Santiago, with the crawdad hanging on, chowing down. When it was just under the surface of the water, we reached slowly under the crawdad with a strainer and scooped it up, water cascading through the strainer with the crawdad caught inside.

Boiled crawdads for dinner with a salad and some pasta. That's my Dad.

Soon after, he taught me to fly fish. I remember standing on his deck on Telegraph Hill, false-casting out into open air toward the Bay Bridge. From there, as the years passed, we started heading to Montana two or three times a year to fish with our guide and friend, Vince Gordon. We fished for trophy Rainbow and Brown and Cutthroat trout in the Yellowstone River, the Jefferson, the Gallatin and the famous Madison River.

Strange analogies maybe, but my Father has thrown figurative bacon wrapped rocks and flies into many streams and rivers the world over and has brought up experiences aplenty, and in this book he writes about them with gusto and zeal, and shares them with us.

It seems that my father has a penchant for being in the right place at the right time. He tells us about seeing Emperor Hirohito in Japan. He tells us about seeing the famous Spanish matador, Antonio Ordonez, *Numero Uno*, on the day he was gored by a bull in Tijuana. He talks about encountering Ernest Hemingway, his own boyhood hero, in Idaho. He even bought a fly rod that Papa Hemingway had owned and he tells us about it in these pages. He writes about visiting Machu Picchu in Peru and Alsace Lorraine, where his own father hailed from. He writes about Venezuela, Malaysia.

Indonesia. Japan. Bali. New Zealand, and Australia.

And within these pages you'll even read about me.

My father got me to read Hemingway when I was a kid. I still read Hemingway today. He had me read Robert Frost and Robinson Jeffers and John Steinbeck. He had me listen to Miles Davis and Dizzy Gillespie, Dave Brubeck and The Modern Jazz Quartet. He had me listen to Bob Dylan. He took me to the Fillmore Auditorium in San Francisco to see and hear Janis Joplin and The Grateful Dead, Jefferson Airplane, and Cream. He took me to performances of the Charles Lloyd Quartet and Charles is our friend to this day.

We have walked the beaches of Hawaii and the beaches of Big Sur together. We have traversed the streets and alleys of San Francisco and Seattle, Hong Kong and small towns and villages in California, Oregon, Washington, Idaho, Montana, and Wyoming.

Together we have eaten some of the best food in the world. In this book he writes about eating huge rib steaks in Montana, and drinking the bile from the gall bladder of a snake in Hong Kong, *Nonya* cuisine, hot with Malay spices, on the island of Penang, and fried clams with creamed spinach in San Francisco.

He even introduced me to a beautiful, young Chinese girl in Hong Kong whom I ended up marrying. My Dad once told me that the world was my oyster and then he proceeded to show me ways to find the pearls inside.

Thanks Dad.

My father is the son of a chef who was the son of an Alsatian baker, and he shares with us his love of food and wine. He is a lover of photography and poetry, jazz and blues, rock 'n' roll and opera. He loves art and architecture, sunsets and landscapes, and he writes about all of this and more with excitement and verve and humor. He is the perfect guide, like our friend Vince in Montana, and takes us on journeys through his exciting world. Climb aboard, my friend, and let's venture forth together.

Orange skies in the east. Lightning over Japan. Rainbow trout "sipping" Baetis flies from the dimpled surface of a river. Roy Orbison. John Coltrane. Kind of Blue. Panama hats. Cold Vodka. Chinese girls.

Thanks Ernie. Lead the way.

–Jeff Beyl

INTRODUCTION

Not long ago I compiled a list of writers, some living, some not, who had nurtured my insatiable desire—need actually—to travel. They are not all travel writers. They are novelists, journalists, and essayists.

What they have in common for me is that after reading them—or I should say re-reading them—I have this almost uncontrollable itch to rise, leave my apartment, and to take a train, plane, boat, even a car, somewhere—anywhere.

My list is long and includes Joseph Conrad, W. Somerset Maugham, Robert Louis Stevenson, Graham Greene, Richard Halliburton, Henry James, Ernest Hemingway, Bruce Chatwin, Kate Simon, Jan Morris, Frederic Prokosch, Paul Theroux, Stanton Delaplane, and others.

Here is my short list of favorite travelers and a few comments about them. If you too suffer from this sweet travel mania, and I'm guessing that you do or you wouldn't be reading this, you probably have your own list of writers that cause this itch I speak of.

The Royal Road

When I was a boy I read Richard Halliburton. After all, didn't he swim in the Taj Mahal pool one moonlit night? Didn't he ride an elephant across the Alps like Hannibal? Didn't he jump into the Mayan Well of the Dead where human sacrifices were thrown to the Rain God? Didn't he swim the 50-mile Panama Canal, treading water as the locks lifted and lowered him to the proper water level?

And, of course, didn't he disappear trying to sail a Chinese junk from Hong Kong to San Francisco?

Richard Halliburton had the itch I talk about. He tells about it in his first book—*The Royal Road to Romance*. I read it when I was in knee pants. Halliburton says he was sitting in his room at college one spring night and was simply overcome by a desire to get away. The next thing he knew he was on his way along the Royal Road to Romance. That's

W. Somerset Maugham on his 75th Birthday. PHOTO: FRED LYON

what this travel itch leads to. In my library I have a first edition of an early Halliburton book—*New Worlds to Conquer*—which was published in 1929. In the front of the book, opposite the title page, there is a photo of Halliburton at the summit of Mexico's Popocatepetl. He is standing there in boots and jeans, his hair blowing wildly. He is steadying himself against the wind with a long staff. And he has a big grin smeared across his boyish face. Of course he is grinning. He is on that Royal Road.

The Asiatics

Years ago, on a troopship crossing the Pacific on the way to Asia, I came across a dog-eared copy of an extraordinary book called *The Asiatics*. I read the entire book during one hot sleepless night while tossing in my bunk. Who could sleep on a troopship anyway? *The Asiatics* is a novel of sorts published in 1935 by a young man named Frederic Prokosch. It describes the adventures of an active young American who hitchhikes from Damascus to Hong Kong. Think of it. That is what the narrator of *The Asiatics* does—hitchhikes across Asia, falling in and out of various troubles and problems, and having a grand time doing so. The book is exceptionally rich in detail, ripe with adventure. It exudes mystery and danger. The landscapes are strange and exotic. Its characters are finely drawn and delineated.

Frederic Prokosch's narrator zig-zagged across Asia in a fascinating route that riveted my attention right through until dawn. And the amazing thing—which I did not realize until much later—the author had never been to Asia. He made it all up—all of it.

Later, in another Prokosch book—*Voices, A Memoir*—his biography, published in 1938, the author comments on how he wrote *The Asiatics:* "One day I was leafing through an enormous old atlas. It was bound in gray buckram and smelled like a mildewed tent. I stared at the coast of Lebanon and saw the hills covered with cedars. I moved eastward toward Syria through the stones and the gorges. The apricot trees stood empty of fruit in Damascus and pilgrims were passing on this way from Transcaucasia."

And so it went, or rather, Frederic Prokosch went in his imagination.

He continues: "Day by day this vision of a continent grew more vivid in my mind. It kept growing in the darkness. It seeped into my dream. I'd wake up in the night with a sudden glimpse of a tropical city, a shabby old hotel, a picnic by the Brahmaputra, and I'd turn on the light and jot it down quickly."

Frederic Prokosch's vision seeped into my dreams as well.

The Dangerous Edge of Things

To me the act of traveling always has a slight edge of the improbable to it, just a *soupcon* of the promise of adventure and possibly even danger. Perhaps that's what has always made reading Graham Greene such a shivering pleasure for me to read. If ever there was a traveler who knew how to milk travel of its promise of adventure it was Graham Greene.

I think back to one of his early books—*Journey without Maps*—published in 1936. In it Greene recounts a harrowing journey through Liberia the year before. He even packed a pistol for that adventure. A certain eerie, studied recklessness persists in almost all of Greene's work. His research for novels took him to West Africa (*The Heart of the Matter*), Haiti (*The Comedians*), Vietnam (*The Quiet American*), always to "the dangerous edge of things," he explains.

But do Graham Greene's works set my mind to wandering toward distant shores? Absolutely! There is only one thing better than sitting at home on a rainy evening reading a book by Graham Greene. That's sitting in the first class section of a Cathay Pacific Airways flight to Hong Kong perhaps, sipping an ice cold, straight-up martini—and reading Graham Greene. Greene credited another travel writer, Norman Lewis, who gave him the urge to visit French Indochina. Greene did and wrote *The Quiet American.*

To Be Duffilled

Paul Theroux is the most intriguing travel writer practicing the craft today. It is also true that he has written a surprising number of first rate novels including *The Mosquito Coast,* and my favorite, *My Secret History.* But it is his works of personal journey I am concerned with here. These are surprisingly unpredictable, witty, gritty, odd, and at times a bit cranky—such as travel itself—and demonstrate what the act of travel does to travelers.

To warm up to the task of writing these few paragraphs about Paul Theroux I browsed through several of his travel books—*The Great Railway Bazaar, The Old Patagonian Express, Riding the Red Rooster, The Pillars of Hercules,* and (as I write this, his latest) *Deep South.*

In *The Great Railway Bazaar*, his account of a meeting with R. Duffill, whose name would later become a verb, is both poignant and hilarious. Just how "duffill" became a verb is explained by Theroux in this amazing and enduring classic.

Theroux was determined to make a grand tour of Asia by train—he didn't pull a Prokosch, but really did it. His route was London to Tokyo and back to London. Paul Theroux is a train person and on this ad-

Paul Theroux. PHOTO: STEVE MCCURRY

venture he tried them all—the Orient Express, the Golden Arrow, the Mandalay Express, the Frontier Mail, the Trans-Siberian, and several "locals."

Why? Because "Anything is possible on a train, a great meal, a binge, a visit from card players, an intrigue, a good night's sleep, and strangers' monologues framed like Russian short stories." Hence *The Great Railway Bazaar*.

But what of Duffill whose name later became a verb?

In *The Great Railway Bazaar* Theroux shared a compartment with R. Duffill on the Direct Orient Express. Duffill, Theroux tells us, was bound for Istanbul. He carried paper parcels bound with string in which he kept, among other things, salami, which he ate in their small, airless compartment. The train stopped at the Italian station of Domodossola. Duffill, Theroux, and a fellow passenger named Moleworth (yes, Moleworth), got off the train and began foraging for food (and wine) in the stalls along the platform. The train began shunting backward and forward. Theroux jumped back aboard. Moleworth followed. But where was Duffill? Alas, Duffill did not make it—thereby creating the verb "duffill" as in to be duffilled or left behind.

If You Haven't Been to Hav
Can You Still Call Yourself a World Traveler?

Here's a quote from the dust jacket from Jan Morris's book *Last Letters from Hav* that was published in 1985: "In the last months before the events of 1984, which irrevocably altered the character of the place, Jan Morris was commissioned by an American magazine to write a series of letters from Hav. She remained there until the end, and this book is the result. It is the first substantial portrait ever drawn of a city that enthralled literary visitors such as Marco Polo, Tolstoy and D.H. Lawrence, but which remained, thanks to its political and geographical attention, virtually unknown to ordinary travelers."

Want to visit Hav? Well, you never will because it exists only in the fertile imagination of travel writer Jan Morris who played the book straight. Thousands of travelers called their travel agents to book flights to Hav. Travel agents called airlines. Airlines called Random House, the book's publisher. Shouldn't there really be a city named Hav?

What follows are some stops I have made along the Royal Road while searching for Hav.

CHAPTER ONE

MISTER EMMRICH'S FROUSY FANNY

When I was ten years old I joined the robins in pulling night crawlers from the back lawn. I used them as bait to catch crappie and bluegill from a nearby urban lake. That was the start of it. I was an angler.

By the time I was 11 I had my first fly rod; a whippy, nine foot, split bamboo monster with a cigar-shaped, cork handle. I was still going after those crappie and bluegill but now I was roll casting into the weed beds near the shore and trying to watch my nondescript, number 10 hook, brown hackle, yellow body. By the time I was 12, I considered myself a full-fledged fly fisherman. I had my own, primitive cast-iron fly tying vise. It was bolted to a workbench in a shack built against my father's one-car garage where he kept the blue, '36 Chevy with the red wheels. At that time there was a small, second-floor fishing tackle shop in downtown Oakland on Broadway. That's where I bought my hooks, thread, hackle, deer hair, peacock herl and silver ribbing. I made up my own patterns. One was something like the old Silver Doctor and it could also fool those crappie and bluegill in Lake Temescal if I let it sink a bit and then jerked it back slowly.

In those days I read a lot about fishing, mostly fly fishing, and I soon was tying standard dry fly patterns like Quill Gordons, but getting the standup wings to stand up eluded me. I tied my flies, read fishing books and hoped someone would take me trout fishing. Then it happened and someone did.

Let's Go Fishing

My introduction into the ranks of trout fishermen was courtesy of my school buddy, Al. To hear Al talk about trout fishing with dry flies was to experience a shiver of excitement that hasn't left me to this day. Al's family had a regular campsite at Bord's Crossing on the

North Fork of the Stanislaus River on the west side of California's Sierra Nevada Mountains. It was up past the former gold mining town, Placerville. One early summer Al invited me to join his family for two weeks at Dorrington, in those days site of a general store with a gas pump and a few broken down buildings. From Oakland we drove with Al's father in a beat up Ford sedan more than half a day to get to there. When we finally arrived, sweaty but excited, we picked up a few things in the store and then drove through a small meadow and turned onto a dusty logging road. We switchbacked down toward the river for two or three miles until we came to an old wooden bridge. That was Bord's Crossing and that's where the Emmrich family had the campsite.

The camp itself, a tent platform, a cooler nailed to a Lodge Pole Pine and a handmade wooden picnic table, sat just above high water near a wide and placid pool where we swam when the sun was on the water and had warmed it up a bit.

Mister Emmrich Skunked Us

That first summer week at Dorrington cemented my devotion to Al and to his father, Mr. Emmrich, a fly fisherman of legendary status with the other campers at Bord's Crossing.

Those two weeks were a learning experience that I have never forgotten. I still draw upon them for what I now call my casting technique and my "reading" of the water. Upstream and downstream from Bord's Crossing, the North Fork of the Stanislaus ran happily along shallows and eddies and sometimes charged through gorges defined by automobile-sized granite boulders. Mr. Emmrich, who had fished that water since he was a young man, had taught Al well, and Al wasn't a bad teacher himself. That is to say, I caught a few small trout early in the first week—six to eight inch browns and the occasional, careless rainbow. Al and I went out early each morning and usually stayed on the river all day, then stumbled back to camp in the dark. Mr. Emmrich never fished with us. He would still be in camp finishing off his morning coffee when we charged off and he was always in camp before we were in the evening. If Al and I went upstream,

Mr. Emmrich went downstream and vice versa. Regardless, he regularly skunked us. He always had a half dozen or more rainbows and browns—12 to 14 inches, sometimes even up to 16. They were beautiful. They were fat and held their color, nestled into wet grass in his bamboo creel. Although Al didn't do badly, he was no match for the Old Man, as we called him, and my fish, at least those big enough to keep and to add to the camp breakfast, always looked thin and puny.

The Frousy Fanny

Even in my anxious state I realized it would be bad form to ask Mr. Emmrich if I could fish with him. But one day after several early hours without a strike, Al and I decided to return to camp for lunch. Later, we were just getting our rods to go out and whip up the water again, when Mr. Emmrich sauntered into camp. He was smiling, but then he always smiled. He swung his creel off his shoulder, handed it to me and hung his rod from the tip on a short broken branch ten feet up on a camp tree.

"How did you do, Mr. Emmrich?" I asked him.

He smiled. "Not bad."

I lifted the lid of his creel and looked in. There were four rainbows that would go 16 inches. They were beautiful.

"What'd you get 'em on?" I asked.

"My Frousy Fanny," he answered.

"What's a Frousy Fanny?"

Mr. Emmrich came over to the tree where he had left his rod and took it down carefully. He walked over to the camp table where Al and I were admiring the fish in his creel. He unfastened his fly from the rod, held it between thumb and forefinger and pushed it close to my nose.

I took it between my fingers, careful not to pull on the tippet Mr. Emmrich was holding. It looked like no trout fly I had ever seen. It looked like a fuzzy piece of heavy gray wool fiber that had been tied in a square knot on the shank of the hook. And that's exactly what it was.

"You caught these trout on that?" I asked. I could hear Al chuckling in the background.

"When nothing else works, my Frousy Fanny always manages to get the fish," he said. "Go get those needle-nose pliers and a number 12 hook out of my tackle box over there and I'll tie you one."

When it Floats I Fish it Dry,
When it Sinks I Fish it Wet

When I had done so, Mr. Emmrich and I sat on opposite sides of the camp table. Al stood watching and grinning. I held up the pliers in my two hands. My forearms formed a triangle and my elbows braced the improvised vice against the table. The pliers clamped the hook leaving the shank exposed.

Then Mr. Emmrich did a curious but memorable thing. He looked down at the front of his lucky Pendleton shirt to a ragged spot along the seam. Several blue-gray woolen fibers stuck out at angles. He reached down and pulled one until he had about four or five inches free. Then, after a quick glance and a smile he wrapped the woolen thread twice around the shank of the hook and tied it off with a square knot. He had good hands for this. Did I tell you that Mr. Emmrich was a jeweler who ran his own shop in downtown Oakland where he repaired wrist watches and created rings and bracelets of gold? With a small pair of scissors from his tool box he cut the ends of the fiber so that about a quarter of an inch remained above the small knot. Then with his jeweler's fingertips he unraveled the short ends of the knot and pushed them around a bit.

"There's your Frowsy Fanny," he said.

It looked like a tiny, grayish, fuzzy bug of indistinct shape.

"This works?" I said incredulously.

"Try it."

"Do you fish it wet or dry?"

"When it floats I fish it dry. When it sinks I fish it wet," he said.

Casting the Frousy Fanny

The next morning, just after sun up Al and I went upstream. Mr. Emmrich was going to go downstream later in the morning. Al crossed over the river on a fallen log and fished a hole that came out from a small waterfall between two large shards of rock. I stayed on the near side and found a slow-moving eddy with an undercut bank. It looked good to me. Needless to say I had tied on my Frousy Fanny. From the bank, I made a few false casts and laid the Frowsy Fanny out at the edge of the eddy. It drifted toward the undercut bank without drag. It was floating. No strike. I kept casting to that spot. The Frousy Fanny floated for a few more casts and then was pulled under at the end of the eddy. I took a few steps upstream and cast to the eddy again. My Frousy Fanny was awash but I could see it a few inches beneath the surface. I thought I saw something move quite near it and, of course, I jerked upward sending my Frousy Fanny into a clump of willows behind my back. It took me 15 minutes to get the tangle out of the willows. My Frowsy Fanny was still okay. I slowly returned to the spot near the bank where I had been standing and made a few false casts. Then I mistakenly dropped my Frousy Fanny out into the faster water and it instantly went out of sight and my line dragged across where I hoped my fish might be. After another two or three casts and I got it right. The drift was good and I could see my Frousy Fanny just below the surface. The fish took it. I managed to land him without too much confusion. A fat, 16 inch rainbow. Or was he 18 inches?

The Stanislaus River

Yes, if your fly floated you were fishing dry. If it sank you were fishing wet. That's the way it was when I was a kid. And I caught fish. Maybe trout were less intelligent than they are now. I don't know.

I tied my own flies. I always tied the same one—gray hackle with a yellow body. I waxed a long piece of black thread from my mother's sewing box and wound it around a number 10 or number 12 hook. Then I wound some heavy yellow silk dubbing over that to form a tiny yellow cigar. Just behind the eye of the hook, I attached a gray, rooster hackle feather, which I wound around stylishly, and then tied it off with a half hitch. A drop of clear fingernail polish right behind the eye finished the fly. That was it. My all-purpose fly—dry or wet. And the trout in the North Fork of the Stanislaus River, between Dorrington and Arnold, loved it.

I also made my own fly tying vise. A pair of needle-nose pliers, held fast in a wood vise fastened to a workbench in my dad's garage. Life was simpler then.

That section of the Stanislaus River in Northern California's Calaveras County where I fished was an interesting stretch of water. Deep, still, frog water in pools where we swam, gave way to merry prankster riffles and braids that gurgled along a gravelly bottom. The river switched and cut back and forth every fifty yards or so and then spilled between giant, eons old, granite boulders, and formed milky pools. I knew there were trout in those pools. I knew it from the bats that darted and skimmed the surface, snapping up the bugs that hovered and flitted about. One early, overcast evening I hooked a bat with one of my false casts. Carrying the weight of my line it dropped into the river and drowned. Afraid to handle it, I broke off the leader and lost my fly.

The section of the river I usually fished was quite narrow. I liked to stand on those boulders where the water tumbled into a nice hole below, dapping my fly gently onto the churning, milky, water below and letting it drift into the clear pool. If my fly floated I was fishing dry. If it sank I was fishing wet. It didn't seem to matter. I had not yet read Izaak Walton's *Compleat Angler*, and this was more than a half century before I would learn about the Japanese Tenkara, dapping method of fly fishing. As a kid I just figured out how to catch fish. And that was one way I did it.

Smoked Trout, Flapjacks and Berry Jam

On a good evening, standing on those boulders and dapping my fly into the water I might catch three or four nice rainbows, all about 13 inches. In those days all trout were 13 inches. I gutted them, washed them in the river and put them in a large side pocket of my Army-Navy store field jacket.

In those days I stayed in a riverside camp with my buddy Al Emmrich and his family. We slept in old, mildewed sleeping bags. We washed in the river. And we hung our fly rods out of harm's way on lower dead branches in a cluster of Douglas Firs. Al's father had built a smoker out of a couple of ten gallon cans. He hung those 13 inch rainbows through their gills in the makeshift smoker on straightened, wire clothes hangers. There was always smoked trout with our camp-fire breakfast of flapjacks with homemade berry jam.

Life was simpler then.

CHAPTER TWO

SHANGHAI 1947

Located on a tidal flat on the left bank of the Huangpu River, Shanghai dates back to the 11ᵗʰ Century and began as a small fishing village along this important Chinese waterway, part of the mighty Yangtze River system. During the 19ᵗʰ Century the city was in the hands of foreign governments that had won valuable trade concessions from the Manchu-Ching Dynasty.

Even today it is easy to see that Shanghai was built primarily by foreigners. It still has the look of a European city—albeit with gigantic skyscrapers. Many of the older buildings that were erected during the foreign occupation, still exist along the broad waterfront street known as the Bund. Today Shanghai is one of the busiest and most dynamic cities in the world. At one time it was estimated there were as many as 60,000 foreigners in Shanghai and they controlled the city—literally. But today Shanghai's past lives only in her museums and antique shops. The present is booming. Where once the Shanghai people were downtrodden and suffered indignities of foreign control, today Shanghai's energetic and urbane people are proud and enthusiastic about life and their place in the modern world.

And that positions us for these tales of Two Women of Shanghai.

My first glimpse of Asia came in 1947, when a U.S. troopship, the S.S. Lejeune, approached the China coast in the dead of night. I was aboard that troopship as a private in the U.S. Marine Corps. I was awake on deck awaiting first light. Scuttlebutt aboard the ship was that the marines would have liberty in Shanghai.

I stood at the ship's railing along with my buddies looking out at an unseen horizon. Ahead was still the blackness of night. But to starboard the blackness gave way to the dark gray of the sea and sky. We were in the mouth of the Yangtze that wound its brown way more than

The author as U.S. Marine on Okinawa. FROM THE COLLECTION OF ERNEST BEYL

3,000 miles through the heart of China. As the sky became lighter I could see a few bulky black shapes through a gray mist on the river. Slowly the Lejeune drew abreast of this dark cluster. Then shapes fell to the stern of our ship and stood out in silhouette—Chinese junks, their high transoms and square ragtag sails against the pearl gray early morning sky. Then there were more junks riding high and ahead of our ship. Then long, low barges could be seen. Then a thin black line of land appeared parallel to our ship's course. And always the big junks were moving up and down the river. At times they passed close by the Lejeune, and men could be seen on their decks, some squatting and gazing back at us. Some were hauling on short lines from the battens, working the tall reddish sails.

A Dutch freighter passed outbound, her hull streaked with rust. A bit later a Danish freighter with a light blue hull and *Copenhagen* printed on her stern, sailed westward along the brown river. Near noon, while a pale sun shined down on the muddy water, the Lejeune stopped briefly mid-river and a small Chinese harbor pilot boarded from a white cutter. He wore a dark, double-breasted suit, and carried a small cloth bag on a strap over his shoulder. Then our ship was moving slowly through a much narrower portion of the river. This was the Huangpu and I traced it to Shanghai with my finger in a small, portable atlas. The junks crowded the smaller river now, their sails bowed in a cross-river wind. It was a cold day and the grayness of forenoon disappeared. A weak sun barely reflected on the river.

Then I began to see the sampans, small wedge-shaped skiffs were sculling across the river. Aboard them figures in black or gray pajamas stood in the stern. They pulled a single long oar set in a Y-shaped brace. The back and forth pulling on the long oar moved the sampan ahead in the water with a clumsy rolling motion. Soon, hundreds of sampans were seen packed against the river banks. Some waddled slowly near the large junks like ducklings near their mother. From time to time a blast from the Lejeune's deep whistle sent them scudding away from the troop transport's bow as we moved slowly up the river. The junks rode high, imperiously in the heavy river traffic. The sampans skittered across the surface like bugs on a pond. Then the Lejeune made a wide turn to starboard around a bend in the Huangpu and there was the harbor and the city of Shanghai.

Rusty freighters rode at anchor or were docked on both sides of the river. Their booms stuck up at angles and tarp-covered cargo was lowered into rocking barges. Squat in the middle of the river an American cruiser lay at anchor. Nearby several destroyers were anchored, their sterns swinging downriver with the current. Small gray landing boats were churning among them, sending brown swirls of muddy water behind. The brooding junks slid up and down the river past the naval vessels and freighters and through thick clusters of sampans like floating leaves. Across the river to starboard the city of Shanghai appeared, a Chinese silkscreen of buildings. Tall apartment blocks, public buildings along the busy waterfront avenue. Double-decked buses moved along slowly. Open-bedded trucks everywhere. Cargo piled along the wharves and up against dock sheds. The Lejeune was almost dead in the water now. There was a jumble of city and waterfront noises—the whir and grind of traffic—horns, whistles, engines, winches, and a babble of voices from the sampans that now edged close to our ship as she stopped in mid-harbor.

The sampans edged closer and closer until one touched the hull of the Lejeune. A small, young woman in gray pajamas stood at stern of the craft. Her one hand worked the single oar lazily to keep the sampan against the big ship. Her other hand was pressed possessively against the hull of the ship. She peered up to the deck where I was standing.

"Hey marine, wanna buy whisky?" she called out.

She had a smile of challenge. Her body moved easily in balance to the small rocking sampan, her outstretched hand flat against the side of the ship. She balanced on one leg for a moment and swung her other leg forward and down, sliding open a small hatch on the sampan's deck. I could see in the shallow hold a dozen or more whisky bottles nestled in a pile of rags. Suddenly the scraping roar of our anchor chain sliding along the ship's side drowned out the woman's shouting. The anchor and its chain hit the surface sending a spume of water into the air. The woman on the sampan was undisturbed.

Near where I was standing at the ship's railing two sailors had thrown a rope over the side. Its end dropped down heavily on the sampan's deck. The woman below smiled, picked up the end of the rope and tied it to small straw basket. She then placed a bottle of whisky in the basket but was careful to hold the rope tightly as the basket sat on the deck of the bobbing sampan. With her other hand she reached out for a long bamboo pole. A small net sack was fixed to one end. Still holding the rope with one hand she pushed the bamboo pole up until it reached the ship's scuppers on the open deck. A sailor grabbed the net sack quickly and dropped silver dollars into it. Then both the sailor and the Chinese woman released their grip and the whisky basket was hauled up on deck. The sale was consummated. Fore and aft along the Lejeune's deck I saw several ropes hanging over the side. Many sampans were edging closer. They bumped and crowded each other for better positions. They were two to three deep almost from bow to stern and more were sculling across the river toward our ship as she rode at anchor. Many of the sampans—unlike the woman's whisky sampan—had small carved lacquer boxes and wooden figures set out on their decks. An old man on one held up a black silk robe with an embroidered pink dragon and let it swing in the breeze. Another man on a sampan stood holding aloft black leather boots.

"Russian boots," he called.

There was a blur of shouting voices from the sampans. But I heard one voice above the others. "Hey Joe, wanna buy whisky?" It was the young woman in the gray pajamas. "Wanna buy whisky, Joe?" she called again. Her hair was shiny black and parted in the middle. A thick black braid hung along her back. She could be 18, I thought—picking my own age—or she could be 30 like the Navy nurses I attempted to encounter on Okinawa—off-limits to enlisted men.

"Now hear this. Now hear this." It was a scratchy voice booming over the ship's public address system. "No member of this ship's company or other personnel aboard this ship will engage in trade with the natives from the deck of this ship. We will repeat this order, "No member of this ship's company or other personnel aboard this ship will engage in trade with the natives from the deck of this ship. That is an order from the office of the deck. That is all." But of course, the trading continued.

Finally, to put a stop to the bartering, the Navy brought out the fire hoses to sweep the sampans away from the ship with powerful jets of water. Suddenly it had become a game. Up on deck the sailors and marines enticed the sampans alongside with shouts of encouragement and promises of sales. And hesitantly, the sampans approached. When they were within range the firehoses released their jets of water and the sampans below were drenched.

The young woman in the gray pajamas was wary. She kept her sampan several yards away from the spray of the firehoses, almost effortlessly moving the single oar slowly back and forth.

"Come on, no water, no water," someone yelled down to her.

She sculled back and forth just beyond reach. Along the deck we—yes, I include myself—called to her, like coaxing a cat out from under a bed. The woman held her sampan steady and looked back at us. There was an uneven smile almost lost in the set of her jaw, and her high forehead showed a frown of doubt. She stood athwart her small craft and placed both hands on the oar. Then she slowly began to pull it one way and push it the other. The sampan glided forward slowly. No one on deck yelled down to her now. She gave a few more tugs on the long oar and the sampan bumped against the side of our ship. But immediately she whipped the craft around and moved off a few yards. She bent over and pulled a bottle of whisky from the tarp on the small deck, keeping her eyes on us above her. She held the bottle aloft and waved it back and forth.

Shanghai Harbor Sampans sail close to troop ship. Hoses from troop ship in Shanghai Harbor drench sampans. PHOTOS: ERNEST BEYL

"Now," someone called softly to the bosun squatting by the hose outlet.

"Hold it for chrissake," someone called out.

The lone sampan with the young woman moved forward again. There was no yelling from our deck. The woman gave another short tug on the oar.

"Hold it," someone said the bosun.

The woman and her sampan were almost to the ship's side. Then her sampan bumped against it gently. She gave one more short pull on the oar and the sampan swung around and rested broadside against the ship.

"Wanna buy whisky," she called out. "Throw rope."

She picked up her long bamboo pole and slowly worked it up to our deck.

"Now," someone yelled. The woman in the sampan had bent to pick up another bottle of whisky.

The International Symbol of Ill-Will

The firehose nozzle was over the ship's side. A thick jet of water shot down and slammed against the woman's back. It knocked her sideways and over into the brown river. Her sampan swung away, bobbing, its oar dragging in the water behind. The young woman, her black braid trailing behind, treaded water for a moment. Then she dog-paddled over to her sampan and dragged herself aboard.

She stood. Her black hair hung wet and heavy along her cheeks, her long braid stiff along her back. Then she placed one hand in the crotch of her soaked pajamas and moved it slowly up and down. She held her other hand aloft toward the deck of the Lejeune. Her fist was clenched but the middle finger was pointed stiffly upward in the international symbol of ill-will. The sampan drifted slowly away from our ship and the woman's middle finger was still pointed to the sky.

CHAPTER THREE

Fish market in Shanghai. PHOTO: ERNEST BEYL

SHANGHAI 1995

I was in Shanghai in 1995 on a business trip. I stayed in a grand hotel, way up on the 30th floor where I looked down toward the Huangpu streaming with maritime traffic. The morning after my arrival from Hong Kong by Dragon Air, I awoke early and decided to go out for a walk before breakfast. As I left the hotel I heard music—not Chinese music but Glenn Miller's "In the Mood." It was coming from across the road where I saw gathered a crowd of several hundred well-dressed Chinese, both men and women. A wide section of the sidewalk had been cordoned off and fifty or more couples were dancing to the recorded music. The rest watched. At 6:30 in the morning these Chinese workers were dancing before bicycling off to work in offices and factories.

A Joint Venture

As I stood watching there was a tap on my shoulder. I turned and an attractive woman in a stylish pants suit said to me in perfect English, "Would you care to dance?" Yes, indeed. I would.

The music had turned to a ballad by Tommy Dorsey and his Orchestra and all around us couples were doing a fine job of ballroom dancing.

"Where are you from?" my dancing partner asked me.

"San Francisco," I replied.

"Ah, San Francisco, what a lovely city."

"Have you been to San Francisco?" I asked.

"No, but I have seen it in the films—*Dirty Harry*, for example. And one day I will go there," she said.

"I hope you will," I said.

"And just what are you doing in Shanghai?" my partner asked me.

"I'm here on business," I replied.

"Ah, joint venture," she said.

And, as it turned out, it was.

CHAPTER FOUR

PICNIC WITH EMPEROR ZHU HOUCONG IN THE VALLEY OF THE MING TOMBS

In the fall of 1982 I journeyed to China with my wife, five-year-old daughter Laurel, and a stuffed toy dog. In those days the Chinese were welcoming visitors, but preferred it if they were part of a group, so they could be managed, and introduced to what Chinese tourist officials wanted them to experience. The four of us (if you count the dog whose name was Theresa) were not part of a group. We booked our own air on CAAC—what the Chinese called their official airline then—and we booked our own hotel reservations at the Jianguo Hotel in Beijing.

The Jianguo Hotel
The Jianguo, operated by the famed Peninsula Group of Hong Kong, was designed by Clement Chen, a San Francisco Bay Area Chinese-American architect. It was a copy of his design for a Holiday Inn in Palo Alto. Why Beijing needed a Holiday Inn remains a mystery. Classic Chinese architecture—the Forbidden City, the Temple of Heaven, and the Summer Palace are exquisite examples of what the vast country has contributed to the world.

After the long flight from San Francisco to Beijing, settling into the Jianguo was like settling into a Holiday Inn, except the service was better and the food went from excellent to spectacular—a trademark of all Peninsula Hotels.

The Jiajing Emperor
But this memoir is not a travel advisory with a star system advising on where to stay while visiting China. It is, rather, an account of a picnic at the unexcavated tomb of Chinese Emperor Zhu Houcong—officially called the Jiajing Emperor —almost 500 years after his death.

One warm autumn day in Beijing wife Joan, daughter Laurel, and Laurel's stuffed dog Theresa, and I decided to go on a picnic in the Valley of the Ming Tombs, site of the mausoleums of 13 Ming dynasty emperors. We had already spent two full days exploring the Forbidden City and the Temple of Heaven. And we made the obligatory walk on the Great Wall. Furthermore, we were all shopped out.

We ordered an elegant picnic lunch from the hotel—cold roast chicken, a green salad, a potato salad, white wine, orange juice, and a chocolate cake, and arranged for a car and English-speaking driver.

The Valley of the Ming Tombs

Mid-morning we were on our way through streams of bicyclists as we drove along Chang An Avenue—a monumental thoroughfare that runs by Tiananmen Square and the Forbidden City. Soon we were slowed to a crawl behind dozens of tour buses all taking tourist groups to the Ming Tombs. Finally, we approached a huge parking lot (many more tour buses) and an adjacent picnic area the size of the 49er football stadium in Santa Clara. It was then, that our driver came up with an unusual alternative.

Spooned and Spooked

It seems he lived in a tiny village in the Valley of the Ming Tombs and offered to drive us there and then to picnic by an unexcavated tomb. We went for it. We drove along a dirt road through a tangle of vines and brush until he stopped the car near a torn, barbed wire fence. We made our way past the fence and interrupted a young couple spooning in the tall grass. We spooked them and they took off on their bicycles over the dusty road.

The Emperor's Temple

We spread a blanket on the ground, opened the bottle of cold white wine, and got out the chicken and the rest of our picnic lunch. In front of us was the tomb of Zhu Houcong, the Jiajing Emperor. We had him all to ourselves. There was total silence except for the buzzing of cicadas. After lunch Joan, Laurel, Theresa, and I explored. A narrow path led to a ten-foot stone wall flanked by stairs leading to the small temple that sat on top of the underground tomb. The temple was faced with a russet-colored wall in which there was an arched opening. In the opening was an 8-foot *stele*, an upright stone slab inscribed with the Emperor's name and details of his reign. The temple was topped by Chinese imperial yellow tiles as are most buildings in the Forbidden City.

The Jiajing Emperor was not a Tranquil Man

When we returned to our blanket for another glass of cold wine our driver told us about this particular Chinese Emperor.

The Jiajing Emperor—Jiajing translates to "admirable tranquility"—was not a tranquil man. He ascended to his rank of emperor at age 14 in 1521 and he reigned until his death in 1567. He ignored state business and early in his reign showed signs of cruelty. He dismissed—or ordered to be executed—rivals and ministers who challenged him. As a youth, because emperors can do anything they set their minds to, he surrounded himself with a bevy of teenage maidens. But he was so rough and demanding they revolted and tried to assassinate him. He survived and ordered them executed by what was known as "death by a thousand cuts"—slowly being sliced to death.

Following the assassination attempt he moved out of the Imperial Palace in the Forbidden City and lived in secret with a 13-year-old girl. Before he died at age 60 he surrounded himself with teenage girls hoping their youth would rub off on him. His death was attributed to mercury poisoning from elixirs he thought would extend his life and his sexual potency. Nice guy!

As far as I can determine—without making a diplomatic, person-to-person call to China's President Xi Jinping—the tomb of the Jiajing Emperor is still unexcavated. Check it out next time you visit Beijing.

CHAPTER FIVE

DUTCH COLONIALISM GAVE US RIJSTTAFEL

Amsterdam is one of my favorite European cities. I've visited several times and used it as the starting point for travels in Holland, Belgium, and Luxemburg. So what do I remember vividly about Amsterdam? Pot! *Haring*! *De Wallen*! *D'Vijff Vlieghen*! *Rijsttafel*!

Yes the Dutch city of Amsterdam is most liberal about its acceptance of marijuana (there is no Dutch equivalent for the word). It's also famous for its raw *haring* (herring), for *De Wallen* (its principal and popular red light district), the restaurant *D'Vijff Vlieghen* (The Five Flies) in five, linked 17th century houses, and *Rijsttafel* (rice table).

Amsterdam is not Gastronomically Notable

With the exception of the herring pedestrians pick up from food stands, dip in raw chopped onion, and then drop them into their waiting mouths, Amsterdam is not gastronomically notable. Nevertheless, there is one Dutch culinary experience that is loved by locals and that visitors seek out. It's *Rijsttafel*. Whenever I'm in Amsterdam I seek out a *Rijsttafel* restaurant and there are several good ones.

So what is *Rijsttafel*? It's an elaborate Indonesian banquet meal of up to 40 or more small plates built around—rice, of course. And it has come down to us as a result of Dutch Colonialism. From 1602 to 1945 Indonesia was a Dutch colony.

Let me quote my friend Fred Ferretti on the subject of *rijsttafel*. Fred is a good man to quote since he was at one time Gourmet-at-Large for *Gourmet Magazine*. I trust him on table matters like this.

Fred said: "The provenance of the rice table is straightforward. In Indonesia a customary meal will consist of a plate of mounded rice and several cooked dishes. All about will be those flavors for which Indonesia is famed—coconut and palm sugars, *trsassi* (a shrimp paste), nutmeg, cloves, any number of sambals, fried onions, and *krupuk* (crisp crackers made of mashed shrimp).

"The importance of spices in the Indonesian kitchen cannot be overstated. Spices have always been Indonesia's riches. Moslem traders were the first to come to the shores of the Hindu, Buddhist, and Indian settlements on the string of fertile islands that were to become the Javanese empire.

"They came for the spices. So did Chinese and Thai traders, followed by the Portuguese and Spaniards, even Marco Polo purportedly the explorer who christened the Indonesian archipelago 'The Islands of Spice.'

"The Dutch were the last to come to Indonesia. At the end of the 16th century they established the Dutch East India Company in the colony they called Batavia. They would be there for centuries, until the end of World War II, cultivating and sending the islands' spices to Holland and the rest of the world."

The Dutch Created Rijsttafel as an Elaborate Banquet

The Dutch seized upon the traditional Indonesian meal and made it into a banquet feast. They called it *rijsttafel* (rice table). But, the *rijsttafel* feast was too elaborate for the Indonesians, too ostentatious. Too Dutch, perhaps—especially after Indonesia gained its independence by standing up to the Dutch after World War II. So today you may occasionally find a restaurant in Jakarta or elsewhere in Indonesia that serves *rijsttafel*, it is not common. Once, on a visit to nearby Singapore, I stayed at the Godwin Park Hotel, and it served a *rijsttafel*.

Most Rijsttafel Dishes are Spicy

But let's move on to what makes a *rijsttafel*.

Foremost, of course, is rice. A large conical mound of cooked rice (sometimes colored and flavored by saffron) is placed at the center of the banquet table. Diners spoon it up and then proceed to surround their rice with sometimes 40 or more "extras"—side dishes—that tempt the palate. Some are hot with chili. Most are spicy. Here are some typical dishes:

Roast Duck—Usually chopped into small pieces and served in banana leaves.

Chicken Coconut Curry—Again, small pieces of chicken served in a mild curry laced with soothing coconut milk.

Spring Rolls—Rice paper rolls filled with shrimp.

Vegetables—Cauliflower, squash, string beans, and bits of potato, sometimes with a peanut sauce.

Bananas—As fritters, or occasionally just as slices of fresh banana.

Satay—Beef, pork, shrimp, or chicken, depending on whether it is Moslem, Hindu or Indian, marinated and skewered on a Bamboo stick and then charred over a small fire.

Peanuts—Laced with chili powder.

Tofu—Sometimes in an omelet, but occasionally in a sauce of chili paste.

CHAPTER SIX

The tomb of Francisco Pizarro in Lima. PHOTO: ERNEST BEYL

THE YEARS HAVEN'T BEEN KIND TO DON FRANCISCO PIZARRO

The city of Lima in Peru was founded in 1535 by the conquistador Francisco Pizarro who ultimately conquered the Incas and brought Christianity to that land. Today a magnificent statue of Pizarro astride his horse dominates a downtown square just off the *Plaza de Armas*. Pizarro was murdered in 1541 by a rival Spanish faction. Small in stature but giant in nerve, there was a time when Pizarro himself could be seen across the plaza in the Lima cathedral. He lay there in a glass case.

Statue of Francisco Pizarro in Lima. PHOTO: ERNEST BEYL

When I was in Lima many years ago on my way to see the Inca citadel of Machu Picchu high in the Andes, I dropped by the cathedral to see Pizarro. I wrote in my notebook then, "The years haven't been kind to Francisco Pizarro."

Then, in 1977, the cathedral uncovered a crypt with a box of bones and a skull. An inscription identified them as belonging to Conquistador Francisco Pizarro. So the good padres removed the unknown "Pizarro" and replaced it with the skull and bones which may now be seen in a glass coffin.

CHAPTER SEVEN

PERU'S PORNO POTTERY

I once made a journey to Machu Picchu, the Inca stronghold in the Peruvian Andes. But before jetting across the mountains to Cuzco and taking a narrow-gauge railway along the Urubamba River to the site of Machu Picchu, I spent a few days in Lima, the Peruvian capital.

I notified the Peruvian tourist officials in advance of my visit so within a few hours of my arrival at my hotel I was contacted by a low-level tourist guide. But I didn't really follow the itinerary she laid out for me. I did a lot of walking around and poked in and out of cathedrals, public buildings, restaurants and bars. That's how I happened on the remains of the conquistador Don Francisco Pizarro.

The Lorca Pre-Columbian Museum

After a day or two my official tourist lady got me cornered in the hotel lobby and said she had arranged a visit to the Lorca Museum. I almost told her to get lost, that I was doing fine on my own but fortunately I didn't. She had a car and we drove out to the Lorca Museum in the Pueblo Libre district of Lima.

The Lorca Museum is a privately-owned establishment of pre-Columbian art. And, if you find yourself in Lima with a free afternoon, go there. You won't be sorry.

The principal collection in the museum which was established in 1925 consists of ceramic and pottery pieces, gold and silver jewelry and other artifacts from 10,000 years of pre-Columbian history.

I dutifully made my way through the museum. I viewed thousands of pottery shards, complete cups, bowls, jars, pitchers, and other cooking items. I viewed and photographed the mummified remains of an ancient Peruvian buried in a kneeling position. There were also crowns, earrings, masks, and nose ornaments. I saw it all.

Inca mummy at Lima's Lorca Museum. PHOTO: ERNEST BEYL

The Porno Pottery Exhibit

Finally, my tour was complete, and I was near the museum's exit and about to thank the curator and take my leave. And that's when it happened.

As we were about to step outside, my tourist guide said something to me I couldn't quite understand. I thought she said something like, "well, that is it—unless you would care to see the erotic pottery exhibit that's not open to the general public." It hit me like a lightning bolt. It was an epiphany—something unexpected, something miraculous. As I said, I didn't quite understand what my guide was saying. I didn't know whether she used the word "exotic" or "erotic", but, on the assumption that she uttered the words "erotic pottery" I nodded my head vigorously in the affirmative.

Those Old Peruvians let it All Hang Out

Well, all right! There it was. Those old Peruvians had let it all hang out. Various forms of sexual activity portrayed in stunning detail.

There they were in pale brown and orange pottery. Twosomes, three-some, and various multiple compilations, imagined and unimagined by this viewer. Gay and straight, there it was. And these were not just drawings in outline on pottery vessels. They were sculptured realistically and displayed in the round. One does imagine that the creators of these marvelous pieces didn't really consider them pornographic. They were simply depictions of ordinary, everyday life. If these artists—for artists they surely were—could see the Lorca Museum today they would wonder why some of their work was under lock and key.

CHAPTER EIGHT

MACARTHUR'S CAR

Following World War II I was a chauffeur in Japan. Yes, a chauffeur. I was a private in the Marine Corps and the driver for Colonel William Fellers, the top Marine Corps officer in the U.S. occupation force in Japan. I drove an old pre-war Plymouth sedan. It was painted Marine Corps green and, for its age, ran fairly well.

One night I drove the colonel and Mrs. Fellers from where we were stationed at the U.S. Naval Base at Yokosuka, to Tokyo to attend a high level party at the old Imperial Hotel which was designed before the war by architect Frank Lloyd Wright. To drive colonel Fellers and his wife to parties in Tokyo was not unusual. Official visits to postwar Japan by a senator, ambassador, commissar or what-have-you, usually called for a party. Brass was polished, dress uniforms pressed, and all the top officers for occupying forces within driving distance headed for Tokyo. It was a duty call. So it was that summer evening in 1947 that I began driving toward Tokyo just at dusk. Then the trouble started.

Dead Battery

As it grew dark I became aware that the headlights on the old Plymouth were becoming dim. The car's generator, I surmised, had stopped generating and I was driving the colonel and Mrs. Fellers to Tokyo strictly on the battery which was being drained as we went along. In those days, shortly after World War II, Tokyo was a barren, dark city, and that night it became very dark until I reached the Imperial Hotel and turned into the long driveway in order to discharge my passengers beneath the Frank Lloyd Wright portico.

Panic at the Imperial Hotel

I found myself in a long line of polished, pre-war automobiles, each

General MacArthur's Car at General Headquarters in Toyko, 1945.
PHOTO: CLIFF MCCARTHY / COURTESY CHUBU UNIVERSITY, FLICKR.COM/ OHIOUNIVERSITYLIBRARIES

inching forward by standard gear shift and clutch, one car at a time, to unload its precious partygoers at the hotel entrance.

"If I kill the motor," I thought, "I am a dead man."

Halfway down the graveled driveway I killed the motor. Of course!

I will skip over the courteous but colorful dialogue that was exchanged between the private and the colonel and cut to the chase, so to speak. The Marine Corps has always had a powerful way of intimidating young privates. I was no exception.

The General's Cadillac

I noted bright lights in my rear view mirror and I heard a distinctive horn that honked delicately but insistently. I pushed the Plymouth's starter button with my foot and heard the characteristic click all drivers came to recognize and fear—dead battery.

In a moment there was a knock at my driver's side window. Although it was summer the windows were rolled up against mosquitos. I rolled down the window and there was General Douglas MacArthur's red-headed sergeant-driver leaning on the doorsill.

General MacArthur and Emperor Hirohito at their first meeting at the U.S. Embassy, Tokyo, 1945. PHOTO: LT. GAETANO FAILLACE / WIKIMEDIA COMMONS

"Get this rust bucket out of the way. I've got the old man back there," the sergeant said softly.

And sure enough, behind me was an ancient Cadillac limousine with five-starred, United States General-of-the-Armies-of-Occupation, Douglas MacArthur, flags waving atop each gleaming fender. A mere mortal, I averted my eyes, just as Japanese citizens averted theirs when Emperor Hirohito's car drove by along Tokyo streets.

I Ask for a Push

What could I do? I politely requested a push from the general's driver. He didn't believe this was a sound idea. Neither did Colonel Fellers. I began contemplating my upcoming life behind bars.

Well, in the end, it all worked out fine. MacArthur's sergeant and Feller's private simply commandeered about 20 Japanese onlookers in the Imperial Hotel driveway and they pushed the Plymouth beneath the portico. I stopped the car with a touch of brake, jumped out, opened the back door, stood at attention, and gave the colonel and Mrs. Fellers my best, fancy, Marine Corps, hi-ball salute as they disembarked. Then my Japanese squad pushed me out of harm's way. The Cadillac followed, stopped beneath the portico and discharged the Five Star General. There were cheers, but I don't remember whether they were for me or MacArthur.

CHAPTER NINE

VISITING EMPEROR HIROHITO

Hirohito, the Japanese Emperor, was the world's longest reigning imperial monarch. Considered divine and a descendant of the sun, a god come down to earth, Hirohito ascended to the Japanese Chrysanthemum Throne on Christmas day 1926. He reigned there until he died in 1989. Mere mortals were not to gaze upon Hirohito, and when his motorcade passed through Tokyo, the Japanese capital, people on the streets bowed and averted their eyes.

General MacArthur Made Hirohito a Mortal

World War II, General Douglas MacArthur, and the political institution of democracy changed all that. And in 1946 Hirohito publically rejected the concept of imperial divinity and became a mere mortal.

After that, twice a year—on his birthday and on January 2nd, the day following the New Year holiday—Hirohito stepped out onto the balcony of a low, modern building on the Imperial Palace grounds and waved to his subjects. The fact that Hirohito became a mortal and displayed himself to his Japanese subjects is an extraordinary thing.

Snaking Along were Thousands of Japanese

In the early 1960s I was roving around Asia as a free-lance writer and on one occasion was in Tokyo over the New Year holidays. I was staying at the Palace Hotel right across a wide boulevard from the Imperial Palace grounds. Very early the morning of January 2nd I awoke—complete with the journalists' mandatory hangover from a New Year's Eve party. There was a strange buzzing in my ears. When I realized the buzzing wasn't coming from inside my skull I stepped to the window and looked out. Below—snaking along slowly as many as ten abreast— were thousands of Japanese.

Japanese Emperor Hirohito on the Imperial Palace grounds. PHOTO: ERNEST BEYL

My first thought was that the city of Tokyo was being evacuated because of some natural disaster such as an earthquake which I had somehow missed in my sleep. I telephoned the front desk for emergency instructions. And that was how I learned about visiting the Emperor.

Waving to the Emperor

A half hour later I joined the throng below. At six feet, four inches, I had a good view and pushed my way ahead until I was within a few hundred celebrants at the head of one section of this slowly moving monster. When we crossed the bridge over the Imperial Palace moat I was literally in the lead of my vast group. A half hour later I was one of about 10,000 enthusiastic early birds that were singled out for the first audience with the Emperor. All of us either waved a small Japanese flag, or held a small Japanese camera, and stared at a balcony fronted by bullet-proof glass. Miraculously I was in the front row.

He Appeared Behind Bullet-Proof Glass

Then, suddenly, a few minutes after 10 o'clock, sliding paper doors behind the bullet-proof glass balcony slowly parted. A small man stepped out onto the balcony and pandemonium took over. There was Emperor Hirohito, five-feet-five-inches tall, in striped pants and a formal tailcoat. He raised his right arm, palm outward, as though he was taking an oath, and mechanically waved it back and forth like a train signal. I waved back and shot a few photos with my small Japanese camera. Behind me was a red froth of waving Japanese flags.

I learned later, Hirohito appeared eight times that day, always behind his bullet-proof shield. (A few years earlier a hothead threw a steel ball in Hirohito's direction, hence the bullet-proof glass.) Japanese police estimated that more than 100,000 persons had entered the wooded Imperial Palace grounds the day I was there and waved at the Emperor.

CHAPTER TEN

ODDITIES AND ODDMENTS

What's the old catch phrase?—Travel is broadening. It may broaden your beam since travel and dining are synonymous, but travel is also enlightening. One picks up a lot of oddities and oddments. Fellow travelers tell you things, and you file them away. Here are a few I have filed away.

Brave Seafarers from Afar

Ancient Polynesian seafarers, bold men and women who probably set out from the Marquesas sometime around 800 A.D., sailed huge, double-hulled canoes carved with stone tools from tree trunks. Pandanus fiber sails caught the winds and the crafts moved northward across the Pacific swells. These Polynesians steered by the sun and at night by the moon and stars. They used stick charts on which their predecessors had "mapped" various Pacific island groups. After thousands of nautical miles they made an important landfall. It was Hawaii where they lived in grand isolation for more than a thousand years—until they had visitors.

Marco Polo and Pasta

At least 50 years before Marco Polo set out on his famous journey from Venice to China, both Indians and Arabs were already eating noodles.

No Horns for the Vikings

The Vikings, those magnificent sailors who rode their sturdy "longboats" on lengthy sea voyages as discovery, adventure and trade, are often depicted today as wearing horned helmets. However, there is no known pictorial record that they ever did wear animal horns on their headgear.

There Really was a Thomas Cook

The name Thomas Cook is almost synonymous with travel and tourism. In 1875 Cook, a "travel agent" organized the first North Cape pleasure cruise. He overbooked a regular postal mail boat, and that prompted him to charter a streamer. But perhaps his most spectacular achievement was not in the realm of pleasure travel at all, but his exploit in transporting 18,000 men up the Nile in 1884 for the attempted relief of General Charles George "Chinese" Gordon who was killed in the siege of Khartoum.

To Burn or not to Burn

Sir Richard Francis Burton, the English explorer, is said to have discovered the source of the Nile. He was a prolific writer throughout his lifetime setting down not only tales of his adventures in Africa and the Middle East, but also translating and annotating obscure works such as *The Book of the Thousand Nights and a Night* which we know today as *The Arabian Nights*. When he died in 1890 his aggrieved wife Isabel agonized over his papers—completed, but not yet published manuscripts as well as unfinished work. Believing them to be pornographic, she burned them.

The White Rajahs of Sarawak

For more than a century Sarawak on the island of Borneo, once the home of headhunting Dyaks, was ruled by a benevolent family of Englishmen named Brooke. The first white Rajah, an adventurer named James Brooke, sailed out from Singapore and up the Sarawak River to Brunei on the good ship *Royalist*.

Later, after Brooke helped quell a pirate uprising, the Sultan of Brunei and his family deeded Sarawak to him for a few thousand Spanish dollars. At one point the tribal Dyaks came to him and asked permission to do a bit of headhunting. Rajah Brooke demurred.

The Oldest Restaurant in Beijing

The Sichuan Restaurant is the oldest restaurant in Beijing. It sits in a hutong—small compound—in West Beijing that was once the mansion of a Qing Dynasty prince. The restaurant is famous for its home-style dishes including Mrs. Pockmark's Bean Curd (*Mapo Doufu*) and is named for the woman who originated it and the bean curd sits in a spicy chili and bean sauce. When I ate in the Sichuan restaurant in Beijing I tried the *Mapo Doufu*. It burned my mouth and numbed my cheeks.

Where is Christopher Columbus?

Christopher Columbus, the Genovese explorer, whom you will remember discovered the western hemisphere in 1492, lies in a magnificent marble crypt in Seville's Cathedral of Santa Maria. But does he? In another cathedral, on the island of Hispaniola, in the Dominican Republic city of Santo Domingo, is a second crypt—with what's left of Christopher Columbus—beneath its principal altar. Both Seville and Santo Domingo claim the authenticity of the remains.

CHAPTER ELEVEN

INCA GHOSTS AT MACHU PICCHU

As a boy I read about Machu Picchu in the *National Geographic* magazine. Actually, I didn't. What I did was to look at the great color photos of Machu Picchu. I confess now that I never read the *National Geographic*. My father gave me a subscription one Christmas long ago and for all those years I scanned the magazine monthly. Most of them were stacked in my closet for decades. The photos of Machu Picchu riveted me. I wanted to go there and I did.

One morning years later I stepped around a stone outcropping and there it was, the last Inca stronghold, 2,000 feet above Peru's Urubamba Valley. The incredible stone ruins of the Inca citadel fell away on green terraces down toward the faraway valley where the white Urubamba River raged. Just beyond the saddle in which the ruins clustered was the namesake of the Inca citadel, Machu Picchu (old mountain), poking its ancient head over the horizon. And a little farther, and higher by far, was Huayna Picchu (new mountain) which a day later I was to climb for a still more spectacular view. Ghosts of ancient Inca priests were all around me. There was no doubt about it.

Cuzco, the Gateway to Machu Picchu

I had flown from Lima over 20,000-foot Andes peaks to Cuzco, gateway to Machu Picchu. At first brown humpbacked mountains appeared to undulate beneath the wingtips of the DC-3. Soon the snow-topped big peaks came into view. They were like old friends. I remembered them from the pages of the *National Geographic*.

Cuzco lies in a dry brown valley at 11,500-feet above sea level. It was founded by the Incas sometime around 1200. It became their capital but was conquered in 1533 by Francisco Pizarro, the Spanish Conquistador.

Cuzco street scene. PHOTO: ERNEST BEYL

Pizarro founded Lima, now Peru's capital, in 1535 with a small band of Spanish marauders seeking gold. They were on horseback. The Incas had never seen horses. They were petrified. Pizarro ultimately conquered the Incas and brought Christianity to Peru.

Today, Cuzco is a highly photogenic Spanish colonial town built on the remains of the Inca stone building foundations. The Incas built without mortar simply fitting stones together by friction—much like a glass stopper in a decanter.

The Conquistador and his followers proceeded to knock down the Inca temples and to build their own churches and public buildings. The Spanish used mortar but their masonry was not as highly developed as that of the Incas. When frequent earthquakes shook Peru, as they have done for centuries, the Spanish buildings toppled leaving the Inca walls and foundations with their marvelous architectural integrity still standing fast.

Several major Inca ruins are located near Cuzco. There are fine guides to show them off. Some are graduates of the archeological department of the University of Cuzco founded in 1621 by the Jesuits. It's the oldest university in the Americas. The most dramatic Inca ruin in the Cuzco vicinity is *Sacsayhuaman*. It was probably an Inca fortress at the time of the conquest. It stands massive today like a sleeping stone giant.

Descendants of the Incas Wear Derbies

There is a large population of Peruvian Indians, descendants of the Incas, in the Cuzco area. They come into town on market days and for local fiestas. Most wear colorful ponchos to guard against frequent cold weather at the extreme altitude. The women wear curious felt hats, snap brim hats, and derbies men wore several years ago and that came back into fashion several years ago with the motion picture *Indiana Jones*. These felt hats worn by the descendants of the Incas, who wore gold helmets and headdresses, vary in color and style from village to village. I envisioned a clever haberdasher from the North stopping off in Cuzco and unloading thousands of felt toppers. To see a Peruvian Indian stroll through the Cuzco marketplace lugging a wooden crate full of scrawny chickens and wearing felt derby, is to suddenly realize an important element about the family of man.

Guinea Pig at the Last Supper

The Indians no longer worship the sun in the manner of their Inca forefathers. Today they are Catholic. In the cathedral bordering the plaza in Cuzco there is a magnificent oil painting by an Indian artist of

The Inca stronghold at Machu Picchu. PHOTO: ERNEST BEYL

the Last Supper. There on the table before Jesus Christ and his disciples is a roasted guinea pig, a Peruvian Indian delicacy.

Along the Urubamba Valley

A narrow gauge railroad still takes most visitors from Cuzco to Machu Picchu. The first 40 minutes of the ride is spent with the train going backward on to sidings, then forward again to negotiate a series of sharp switchbacks too bent for the train to curl through going forward only. Then, deep into the Urubamba Valley, visitors leave the train and ride mini-vans up to the sacred and improbable Inca stronghold. That's what it was, a stronghold. Machu Picchu was one of a series of Inca positions guarding the access routes from the tropical jungles of the fierce Antis (a savage tribe frequently at war with the Incas) to Cuzco, heart of the Inca Empire. Machu Picchu was probably constructed in the 15th Century. When the terrible Pizarro and his men captured Cuzco the Incas retreated to Machu Picchu, the inaccessible stronghold high above—and near to the gods of the sun. The Spaniards never did find Machu Picchu, but they did manage to trick the last Inca King, Tupac Amaru, down from the mountaintop where he was captured and executed. From that moment Machu Picchu began to fade. The Inca priests, handmaidens, and workers were doomed. It was the end of the line for them—literally.

The Place Where They Tied the Sun

Gradually, Machu Picchu became only a memory. At one time the Incas may have ruled an advanced empire the size of that of the Caesars. They did it without the wheel, iron tools, or a system of writing. Yet, the granite blocks of their temples and dwellings were cut so perfectly they didn't need mortar.

One carved outcropping at the high section of the ruins was *Intihuatana,* "The place where the sun is tied." It allowed the Incas to predict the solstice and equinox.

Hiram Bingham Finds Machu Picchu

It was not until 1911 that an American, Hiram Bingham, under sponsorship of the National Geographic Society, publishers of that magazine that spent many years in my closet, discovered the wondrous lost city high in the Peruvian Andes.

I spent a night in a small lodge right by the ruins of Machu Picchu. That night I set my wristwatch alarm for four in the morning. When the alarm awakened me I dressed quickly in the cold dark, made myself a cup of tea, and set out. By moonlight and with a small flashlight I picked my way through what, in an earlier time, had been the stronghold's main street. On a small rise I easily found *Intihuatana*, the place where the Incas "tied" the sun. I went beyond it. Found a trail and climbed down into a heavily wooded saddle. Then, as I had been told I would, I found another trail leading upward. An hour-and-a-half later, on the summit of Huayna Picchu, I sat and looked back and below to the Inca ruins. The early morning light fell on them now and although I could not see them, I knew the ghosts of the Incas were present.

CHAPTER TWELVE

Chinese junks in Hong Kong Harbor. PHOTO: ERNEST BEYL

DISCOVERING HONG KONG

Red Sun Over the Peak

One early morning in the 1960s I sailed into Hong Kong Harbor (Fragrant Harbor in the Cantonese dialect) aboard the P&O-Orient Lines ship S.S. Orsova. I had visited Hong Kong before and now I wanted to reestablish contact and get my batteries charged. As we glided slowly toward the old dock on the Hong Kong mainland city of Kowloon, our ship was greeted by a small fleet of sampans, sculled by Chinese women who jerked their small crafts along with a single oar mounted in the stern. I stood on the Orsova's deck and watched a giant red sun rise over Victoria Peak across the harbor.

The romance and mystery of the Orient awaited. There were exotic staircase streets to climb, teeming with vendors. Narrow alleys housed silk and jade merchants, calligraphers, stone "signature" chop carvers, sellers of tiny songbirds, spices, and nostrums.

The Lobby of the Pen

That same afternoon I found the shop of bespoke Indian tailor, Harilela, and was fitted for a tan gabardine, double-breasted suit I would later only occasionally wear. As several members of the Harilela family played me lovingly like a violin, I sipped a scotch and soda and looked at my wonderful soldier-of-fortune, world-weary self in a full length mirror. That's what you did in those days in your Hong Kong tailor's shop.

Later I made my way to the sanctified Lobby of the Peninsula Hotel. That is also what you did in those days. I asked for a table on the right side of the Lobby facing the front desk—the good side. It was separated from the left side (Siberia) by a broad promenade leading to the great old hotel's check-in, concierge, mail desk, and telephone desk. In those days you booked your overseas telephone calls with a striking Chinese woman at the telephone desk. Then you sat in the bustling Lobby and had your second scotch and soda of the day while waiting to be paged for the telephone call you had booked. There was a special "cabinet" or booth in which you took those calls. Could there be anything more grand than the Lobby of the Pen? I can still hear in my mind's ear that murmur of Cantonese and English and the delicate clinking of crystal and china in that vaunted space.

To be paged in the Peninsula Lobby by a young Chinese bellman in a tight white uniform topped with a pillbox cap, who hurried through the grand room ringing a bicycle bell to gain your attention, meant you were "somebody." You had arrived at wherever it was your mind advised that you should be going. The bicycle bell and a small black board with your name chalked on it were mounted on a broomstick the bellman displayed. For me the Lobby of the Pen was (still is) one of the world's grandest spaces—a cathedral.

The Return of Ted Bear

For many years Hong Kong hotels epitomized for me the *luxe* life. The Peninsula had that glorious Lobby and those young bellmen paging you there. The Mandarin Oriental on the other side of the harbor on what we liked to refer to simply as "The Island," usually whisked you around in a Mercedes driven by a crisply uniformed chauffeur. Of course the Pen had its own fleet of Rolls Royces, each one British racing green. A few years later, The Regent had a fleet of Daimlers and that incredible view of Hong Kong Harbor and Victoria Peak beyond. It also played host to Ted Bear.

In the late 1980s I was engaged by the Hong Kong Government in a public relations capacity in the U.S. during the run-up to Hong Kong's date with destiny in 1997 when it would be dramatically turned over to the People's Republic of China. I found myself flying Cathay Pacific Airways to Hong Kong every month or two. On one occasion I took my wife and daughter with me. In those days daughter Laurel always traveled with a stuffed bear—Ted Bear by name. On that trip Laurel slept in a rollaway in our harbor side room at The Regent. One morning Ted Bear slept late while the rest of us went out. The room was cleaned and the sheets were changed. Of course! When we returned later that day—no Ted Bear. There was much crying and wringing of hands. Civilized life, as Laurel had come to know it and expect it, was perhaps over. Or so it seemed. Ted Bear, Laurel knew, was now history—residing somewhere in a Hong Kong dumpster.

But perhaps, just perhaps! A call was made to the resident manager. Ted Bear is missing. Soon a charming young Chinese man wearing the regulation uniform of striped pants and tail coat appeared at our door. The situation was explained. Ted Bear was described in exacting detail. The search was on.

In less than an hour there was a discreet knock on our door. The same young man stood there, this time with several smiling colleagues, some in rough work clothes. In the young man's arms was a slightly damp, freshly laundered, Ted Bear.

Ted Bear has since retired. He no longer travels with Laurel, but reclines on her bed.

Sir Horace and His Ivory Collection

The name Kadoorie is legend in Hong Kong. The Kadoorie family, from Lebanon, fetched up in Shanghai in the city's heyday and made its mark and its millions. Before Mao Zedong triumphed the Kadoories had fled to Hong Kong. There they built a business legacy that remains to this day: Hong Kong and Shanghai Hotels, Ltd., of which The Peninsula is the jewel in the crown, China Light and Power, and so it goes.

Two brothers, Lawrence and Horace Kadoorie, were enormously influential in Hong Kong when I was visiting regularly. Lord Kadoorie (Lawrence) died several years ago. His brother, Sir Horace, died a few years earlier.

On one trip to Hong Kong—"On Her Majesty's Service"—back in the 1960s—I was invited to meet the brothers in their elaborate offices in the St. George Building in "Central" on the "Island," shortcuts always used for the business district in the city of Victoria on Victoria Island, as opposed to the city of Kowloon on the Chinese mainland across the harbor.

I presented myself at exactly the appointed time and was ushered into Lord Kadoorie's presence. An imposing figure of a man, beautifully tailored, with charming conversational abilities, we talked for a while about the future of Hong Kong. That's what everyone in Hong Kong talked about then—as now. Then a door opened and Sir Horace entered. He was in a wheelchair pushed by a strikingly beautiful young Chinese woman in a fine designer suit. Introductions were made. I was presented as somebody or other. My companions on this visit to Hong Kong who were benefactors of San Francisco's Asian Art Museum, had arranged my meeting with the Kadoories. When I mentioned my companions with the Asian Art Museum that was good enough for the Kadoories. Sir Horace, I was told, would show me his legendary, but not publicized, ivory collection. Sir Horace was not an ivory hunter. This was before we were enlightened about ivory and the cruelty and endangerment of the elephant.

We went by elevator to another floor in the building. The elevator doors opened onto what I took to be an unoccupied hallway. Sir Horace wheeled his way to an unmarked door. The young woman with him then pressed a few numbers into a keypad on the wall. The door slid silently upward to reveal an inner steel mesh barricade. Another code was entered on the keypad. The steel mesh barrier slid away to reveal a small vault perhaps ten feet wide and 25 feet deep. We entered. A switch was flicked and there was Sir Horace's ivory collection.

Sir Horace then rolled his way from one secure case to another. There on glass shelves reposed wondrous, intricate, delicate pieces of ivory sculpture—Chinese pagodas, junks under sail, animals, humans, songbirds, castles, tiny scenes hardly larger than a grain of rice (magnified to reveal a rich tableaux), gods and goddesses from the Chinese pantheon, enumerable effigies of Buddha. The striking young woman directed the tour of the vault, speaking earnestly, if a bit mechanically, about some of the choicest pieces. Sir Horace sat in his wheelchair smiling. From time to time he spoke in a small scratchy voice about one or the other of his treasure pieces. He told us that he had spent a lifetime searching for and buying the ivory pieces in this incredible collection but had nearly lost it. I leaned close to his wheelchair to hear him tell his story.

When the Japanese advanced to Hong Kong in 1941 Horace Kadoorie turned his priceless ivory collection over to a trusted agent who somehow managed to escape the British colony with the ivory and take it to Europe before it would have been confiscated by Japanese occupation forces. The Kadoories rode out the war during which time Horace had only sporadic contact with his ivory agent. After the war with the Japanese was over in 1945 Horace waited a bit. The war in Europe had ended as well. Things were looking up and Horace wanted his ivory returned to Hong Kong. But the collection had disappeared, along with the trusted agent.

Sir Horace told me he spent several years (and countless dollars, one assumes) to track down his collection. He didn't tell me how this was done. He allowed only that most of the collection was finally returned to him. Now it hides in a double-locked vault in the St. George Building in "Central" on "The Island." Or at least it did last time I checked.

Hong Kong street scene. PHOTO: ERNEST BEYL

Government House and the Gorilla

One year I covered the Hong Kong Arts Festival for an American magazine. That's how I happened to find an elaborately engraved invitation awaiting me in my room at The Peninsula.

His Excellency the Governor of Hong Kong and Lady MacLehose
Request the Pleasure of the Company of
Mr. Ernest Beyl
At a Reception Government House
In the Presence of
H.R.H. Princess Alexandra
Patroness of the Hong Kong Arts Festival
Black Tie
R.S.V.P. Social Secretary

I telephoned Government House to accept. The social secretary was delighted. And, by the way, would I mind escorting a fellow American journalist, also from California, who was staying at the Pen. I would be delighted.

The next evening I appeared in the Lobby in my rented tuxedo and the dress shoes I borrowed from the hotel's general manager Felix Bieger. I was aware immediately of an unusual buzz in the huge lobby chamber, a collection of murmurs of astonishment. I thought it might have something to do with my rented tuxedo until I realized almost everyone in the Lobby had turned toward the massive glass entrance doors and was staring. There I saw my fellow American journalist (I recognized her from other encounters) waiting for her escort.

The woman was exceedingly attractive. Her hair was a smooth golden cap. Below was her smiling face, appealing. And below that was the body of a shaggy gorilla. That is the only way to describe what I was seeing. I was stopped, astonished, mesmerized. What could this be? Obviously this was my date for the Government House reception. Did she think it was a costume ball?

Then, suddenly, a chord of remembrance, like a brief fanfare, hit me. I had seen that same gorilla a few months earlier in a fashion photo spread in Life Magazine. One of the biggest Paris fashion names had designed a pants suit which, when worn by the model in the magazine, looked like nothing more than the body of a large, black, furry gorilla. The year was 1997. You can look it up in Life Magazine. Now, right here in the famous Lobby of the Pen was my very own gorilla. And my date brought it off beautifully. The shiny yellow cap of sleek hair, the attractive tanned smiling face. She set the outfit off nicely with a single strand of Mikimoto pearls. My gorilla kissed me on both cheeks.

Arm in arm we left the Pen Lobby and its murmurs and entered one of the hotel's chauffeur-driven, British racing green Rolls Royces for the drive to Government House. Why not, I thought, settling back into the rich leather interior. I am blessed.

As we crunched over the gravel entranceway to Hong Kong's Government House, a starchy military aide in white jacket, medals, and a reddish mustache ran to the car and, the moment we stopped, opened the door and stood waiting at attention. My gorilla disembarked. To his credit, the military aide's recoil was minimal. We swept through the imposing entrance into a receiving line with the cream of Hong Kong society—Chinese bankers, British civil servants, Swiss hoteliers, Indian merchants, sleek Chinese and Caucasian women.

And so it was: a lady gorilla comes to Government House with an escort in a rented tux and Felix Bieger's dress shoes.

Again that low murmur. Governor and Lady MacLehose brought it off beautifully (no recoil) and soon introduced us to Princess Alexandra. The Princess was royally gracious. After a fast glance and a smile my way she turned to my gorilla companion to engage her in conversation. The Princess loved California—home to both my gorilla and me. She hoped to visit there one day soon. Was this our first visit to Hong Kong? Would we be attending performances of the Hong Kong Arts Festival? The Princess's gaze was steady. It never dropped below my gorilla's mischievous eyes. And, in spite of the rented tux and borrowed shoes, I think I brought it off.

Dinner with My Tailor

Mr. and Mrs. Peter N. Harilela
Request the Pleasure of Your Company
At Dinner Honoring
Mr. David Roads
Chief Information Officer
The Hong Kong Government

Amazing! An invitation to dinner from my Hong Kong tailor of long ago. How nice of him to remember that tan gabardine suit.

David Roads, an American expatriate friend, was retiring from service with the Hong Kong Government. At the time he was one of two Americans in "Her Majesty's Service" for Hong Kong. I was the other American but served in the U.S. The Harilelas were having a retirement party for David Roads in their home on Waterloo Road in Kowloon. There were a lot of Harilelas and they all lived in a vast and ornate house—actually the Hong Kong version of a palace.

After I arrived and was greeted I was invited to join other guests on a tour of the grand building, a kind of compound with separate and elaborate quarters for Harilela sons and daughters-in-law, for daughters and sons-in-law, for swarms of children. We guests made our escorted way through the four-story building. A vast ballroom. A playroom the size of a school gymnasium for all the Harilela kids. A large cafeteria—staffed 24-hours a day, we were told. Roomy apartments (which in turn had their own kitchens), living rooms, bedrooms, day rooms and on and on.

Not bad for a bespoke tailor.

It was, as they say, an occasion. Beautifully gowned Chinese women speaking perfect King's English chatted with their partners and escorts. A smattering of British civil servants speculated on Hong Kong's future. American stockbrokers spoke of the Hang Seng Index. Officers from the Royal Navy were splendid in their uniforms and medals. A senior man from the Hong Kong Police Force chatted with someone from the Hong Kong Narcotics Bureau, and a top editor from the South China Morning Post was deep in conversation with a priest known to have access to people across the border in the People's Republic of China. Many of the elegant women held positions of responsibility and power in the Hong Kong government or in business. As Chairman Mao said, "Women hold up half the sky."

A uniformed page walked through the drawing room where we were gathered ringing chimes that called us to dinner as one would expect on a vast cruise ship. We entered an enormous dining room, as large as that of a large luxury hotel. There, hanging from the high ceiling, in the precise center, was a chandelier the size of a sci-fi movie space station. Beneath it was the largest round table I had ever seen outside of New York City's UN Building. It floated in the great room like a gigantic white cloud. The whiteness of its giant table cloth was blinding. The silver cutlery and candleholders were enormous.

Uniformed waiters bustled about pouring glass tumblers with Johnny Walker Red Label Scotch. Champagne bubbled in fine, incredibly thin glass flutes. There was Russian vodka, of course. And all of this even before the first course was even served. I recall Chinese birds' nest soup and other Chinese dishes. Indian delicacies followed one after another and included a mild curry served with true silver leaf sparkling through the rice. I asked about the recipe and a few moments later it appeared at my place in a monogramed envelope.

And that's the way it was at David Roads's retirement party.

Let's Drink to Absent Friends

My friend the Hong Kong-based foreign correspondent Richard Hughes— who borrowed the phrase "Borrowed Place, Borrowed Time" for the title of his book about Hong Kong from Chinese author Han Suyin—held court frequently for visiting journalists at the Hong Kong Foreign Correspondent's Club, known by everyone as the FCC. I was there occasionally as a guest member with my friend Kevin Sinclair, then a columnist for the South China Morning Post. Both Hughes and Sinclair were legends in Far Eastern journalistic circles.

Usually, after a lengthy afternoon session of gin and tonics, Hughes would ask the bar steward for a stack of FCC postcards and then request all of us in the group to name absent friends. Each would come up with a name. To those who had already departed this mortal coil we lifted our glasses in tribute. And for those who were simply absent from Hong Kong that day, but not absent from our thoughts, we remembered with a postcard which all of us signed with flourishes. Then Hughes requested the bar steward to post them.

I wish I was there at the FCC now drinking to absent friends and signing postcards. Richard Hughes himself has gone, departed, departed from Hong Kong and from this world. Kevin Sinclair is gone too. I believe Felix Bieger is still with us. I hope so. And, I haven't heard anything from David Roads in years. I don't know whatever happened to my lady gorilla, but I do see Ted Bear now and again.

CHAPTER THIRTEEN

ALSACE-LORRAINE: IT'S ALL IN THE FAMILY

Only about 100 miles separate the crown jewel Alsatian city of Strasbourg, and Lorraine's classic capital, Nancy. Yet, over the years a strong allegiance to their chosen cultural history has separated friends and even families in this northeastern region of France. My family was one of those separated.

Waverley Root, in his monumental book, *The Food of France*, said "Alsace-Lorraine is a word whose two parts seem destined to remain tied together by their hyphen, but their conjunction is more or less an accident of history."

Both intermittently part of Germany or France since the Middle Ages, Alsace and Lorraine at times shared either French or German sovereignty; at others times, Alsace was German territory and Lorraine, French.

A Visit to Strasbourg

My father Joseph was born in the now-French province of Alsace and as a youngster immigrated to the United States. I was familiar with his homeland through his many recollections and through books on Alsace he collected and I now treasure. One has a watercolor reproduction of his 17th Century, half-timbered family home in the Alsatian village of Obernai. On the ground floor was the family bakery. When my father died I became the patriarch of the American branch of my family and had a strong urge to visit my roots. So a few years ago in late summer, with my wife and daughter, I set out for a sentimental visit. At the time my father's sister Anna lived in Strasbourg where I still have cousins. Other cousins lived then in nearby Lorraine just across the Vosges Mountains, and there were various nieces and nephews in both Alsace and Lorraine.

My Father the Chef

When my father came to the U. S. in 1912 as a youth, both Alsace and Lorraine belonged to Germany, just to the East across the natural boundary of the Rhine River. My father, the son of an Alsatian baker, became a U.S. citizen, married and became a chef. He spent the rest of his long life in and around San Francisco with only two short visits to his Alsatian homeland. His older brother Leo immigrated to France and joined the army. Later, he too became a chef. He married, had children and lived out his life in Lorraine. As my always Germanic father would say later, "Leo became Frenchified."

Two Different Cuisines

On my visit I found much more than the Vosges Mountains separating the Alsace and Lorraine branches of my family. Those relatives living in Alsace, while French, of course, but they also frequently spoke German and a patois known as *Alsacienne*. The Lorraine family contingent was totally French in spirit, style, and language. I found that much of this difference was expressed in the food they served at home. It was as different as…well, the French and German languages. So this is a personal tale of two family cuisines, if you will.

Alsatian Cookery

There are many fine restaurants in both Alsace and Lorraine; some with Michelin stars and international reputations. The food served is French haut cuisine although some Alsatian specialties are found as well. But family fare in Alsace and Lorraine remains closer to traditional dishes of each province and tends to differ sharply. Alsace is famed for its hybrid, German-style dishes such as *choucroute garni* (sauerkraut with potatoes, smoked pork, various sausages, and even goose at times). The home cooking of Lorraine aligns more closely with traditional French country fare.

Sauerkraut and German Beer

During the Alsatian days of this journey we enjoyed a memorable meal with my aunt Anna and cousin Freddy whose wife Ginette was our cook. This meal was a textbook example of Alsatian-style cookery. The lengthy, at-home luncheon consisted of an appetizer of *pate de foie gras* served with an Alsatian Gewürztraminer. This was followed by a huge platter of *choucroute garni* (sauerkraut, carrots, potatoes, smoked pork and several kinds of local sausage and was accompanied by frosted steins of German beer. Then followed two cheeses, a strong Munster and a soft and creamy St. Hubert, which we ate with homemade, brown bread. Dessert was the traditional *kugelhopf*, a light golden, round cake baked in a tinned form with a hole in its center. The cake was dusted with powdered sugar. There were also cookies, blueberry pie and home-made ice cream with *framboise* sauce. Not your typical light lunch.

A Visit to Thorey Lyautey

We spent a week in Alsace, then asked my aunt to telephone ahead (approximately 100 miles) to my cousins in Lorraine to advise that the following morning we would be on our way for a visit that had been previously established by letter. My Alsatian aunt declined saying that the two branches of the family were "not close"—a personal example of how Alsace and Lorraine is a land divided. My daughter Laurel in her best schoolgirl French made the call and the arrangements for our next family meeting. And so we drove to Lorraine for a visit with my relatives who lived in Thorey Lyautey, a tiny village near Nancy.

We were welcomed warmly by my cousin Renee, her husband Roger, and their German Shepard who led us on a tour of the garden. Renee picked long waxy *haricot jaune* (yellow string beans) and dropped them into the apron tied around her waist.

The festive early evening meal consisted of typical French country food. First we sipped some of Roger's celebratory homemade eaux-de-vie Mirabelle he made the year before. Then the meal began with these appetizers: a homemade vegetable terrine, crackers with thin slices of garden tomato topped with slices of hard-boiled egg with a dot of homemade mayonnaise, bread from a village bakery, sweet butter and gherkins. With a nod toward the other side of the Vosges Mountains, this was served with a glass of Alsatian Pinot Blanc. Then followed a roast loin of pork (slightly pink) with a small *Quimper* pitcher of au jus.

The *haricots jaune*, sautéed with bacon bits, accompanied the roast. This was served with a modest Cote du Rhone. Next was a garden lettuce salad with a mustard vinaigrette (No wine with the salad). Three cheeses followed: Camembert, St. Albert, and Port Salud with the remaining wine—and again there was bread with sweet butter. Finally there were fresh white peaches and purple grapes—again from the garden. After dinner we sipped tiny glasses of eaux-de-vie Mirabelle.

On parting, Roger gave us some of his eaux-de-vie in a brown whiskey bottle stopped with a cork. Later that night in our hotel room back in Nancy I sipped some of it before I went to sleep and left the glass on the nightstand by the bed. The next morning the room was perfumed by the scent of golden plums.

Today, much of the world's cuisine is homogenous. Let's hope the traditional family cuisines of Alsace and Lorraine retain their individuality. And the passage of time has eased the awkward separation. These days my relatives in Alsace are comfortable with telephoning family members—and even traveling across the Vosges Mountains for a visit.

CHAPTER FOURTEEN

BUNG SUKARNO'S MAN

Early in the 1960s I wrote a letter to the Republic of Indonesia's President for Life, Achmed Sukarno. He was the man who fought for Indonesian independence following World War II and wound up leading one of the most populous nations in the world into a tough, pro-communist stance. He was later stripped of his power in an Indonesian army revolt.

I was about to embark on a journey to Southeast Asia as a free-lance journalist and I wanted to interview Sukarno and to see how he was doing with his more than 3,000 islands of the Indonesian Republic.

I knew an American photographer, Johnny Floria, who, following World War II, had covered the Indonesian freedom revolt for Life Magazine. When I told Johnny Floria I was going to Indonesia he said, "Look up my buddy Bung Sukarno." In the Indonesian language the word "Bung" is an honorific title tantamount to big brother.

So I wrote a letter to Achmed Bung Sukarno, President of Indonesia. I wrote that I would be in Jakarta on a certain date and requested an audience. Sukarno did not reply—at least as far as I could discover. And I left for my trip.

I bummed around Southeast Asia for several weeks with my friend, a photographer named Arthur Adams. We spent some time in Hong Kong, then flew to Bangkok, hunkered down there for a while, then flew on to Kuala Lumpur and a few intermediate stops. Art and I finally established ourselves in a small hotel in Singapore called the Cockpit where a lot of journalists hung out. It was too hot to wear trench coats (as all journalists were supposed to do in those days), so the uniform of all journalists in Singapore was a short-sleeved cotton shirt and khaki pants. That's what Art and I wore day in and day out. And we dined on *rijsttafel* with Tiger Beer at the well-named Cockpit. After a few weeks, we tired even of this hedonistic routine and headed for Jakarta with cheap tickets on Garuda Airlines.

We were gathering our bags in Jakarta's airport when we met a tall, handsome Indonesian who also seemed to have just arrived in the capital, and who, in a good-natured and helpful manner—"greased us" through customs and immigration. He joined us in the taxi to our hotel. In fact he was staying at the same hotel, he said. The following morning he appeared at breakfast. Meanwhile, I tried to telephone Bung Sukarno about the interview but was unable to get through the clutter of underling and officialdom. Later in the day we ran into our handsome Indonesian friend at a restaurant Art and I had selected for lunch. That evening the same thing happened. It was just a coincidence. We laughed at it over a Tiger Beer. For several days the coincidences mounted. Even at that time Jakarta was a city of a million or more Indonesians.

On the spur of the moment Art and I decided to fly to Bali. Believe me it was on the spur of the moment. That's the way we did things in those days. It took us four days to get a flight out to Jogjakarta with a connection to Denpasar on the Island of Bali. The flights were always commandeered by officers of Sukarno's army.

On the fourth day, at the terminally crowded terminal at Jakarta International Airport, our tall Indonesian friend, who we now called "George," much in the same fashion that the Beatles called their haircuts "Arthur," this time "greased us" past a contingent of soldiers we believed were set to commandeer the airplane. We waved goodbye to George and boarded.

We made it to Denpasar and took an ancient taxi to the Sanur Beach Hotel. And while we were having a Tiger Beer in the thatched roof welcoming area in walked George. What a surprise! What a coincidence! And that's the way we always played it with George. One evening over many Tiger Beers, Art and I hiked over to a Balinese village for an all-night dance performance. Of course, we ran into our buddy George. It was at that point that I finally asked, "Why are you following us around Indonesia?

"Who's following you around Indonesia?" George asked in precise English.

"Did Bung Sukarno ask you to follow us and look after us, and maybe to make sure we don't get in trouble?"

"Who's Bung Sukarno?" George said.

I may have been overplaying our meagre hand in that exchange and we didn't see George for several days after that. Art and I boarded a Garuda flight back to Jakarta without any difficulty. We spent one more night at a hotel there. No George!

The following morning we went to the airport. It was a nightmare come true. Customs and immigration procedures were endless. Money that had been declared on entry to Indonesia now had to be accounted for in detail. This was nearly impossible for us since street-smart money changers abounded and fantastic deals were available to those who had U.S. dollars. Tedium prevailed. Officialize dominated. Presumed problems were set forth in excruciating detail. Problems with the authorities were not to be taken lightly we were told. We could be jailed, we were told. This news drifted through our minds like a noxious vapor (remember this was in the early 1960s).

Then, suddenly there was our George. Tall! Smiling! Confident! "Wired!" And George was displaying extreme 'juice" with the armed officials.

"Well, what a coincidence," he said to us as we stood in a tiny room in the "secure" immigration area. "My friends, you are leaving Indonesia? What a pity."

And then, after a few words from George we were released and sent on our way. We walked out to the unbelievably hot and sticky tarmac, up to the airplane door, entered to the unbelievably hot cabin, and soon were bound for Hong Kong.

Later, back in San Francisco, I wrote another letter to Bung Sukarno thanking him for his many courtesies when Art and I were in his country. And I asked him to give my regards to George. I never received a reply.

CHAPTER FIFTEEN

A Hindu temple on the Island of Bali. PHOTO: ERNEST BEYL

BALI: THE MORNING OF THE WORLD

Reflections following a visit to the Island of Bali:

On the glorious, green, Indonesian, jewel island of Bali, it would seem that everyone is an artist, or a patron of the arts, or perhaps even, an art critic. To the Balinese art is always. Art is everything.

Miguel Covarrubias, the late Mexican writer-illustrator who wrote the definitive book on Bali, *The Island of Bali*, called the Balinese "…an elegant and decorative people…living in close harmony with nature." Covarrubias, who had a broad knowledge of art archeology, ethnology, and anthropology, visited the beautiful Indonesian island many times, and he expressed this concept of the Balinese oneness with artistic expression.

The Balinese Themselves are Living Sculpture

Almost every Balinese village has its own classical dance troupe, its own traditional *gamelan* (orchestra). Its own opera company, as well as intricately-carved Hindu temples, and statues of pantheistic and sometimes animalistic gods and goddesses.

Balinese women craft magnificent offerings to these gods and goddesses made from rice (a symbol of life to them), fruit, flowers, and even chili peppers. To see these women walking along a trail to the local temple, straight of back, and balancing a towering temple offering on their heads, is to exult on a piece of moving theater, or perhaps, a living sculpture. Art indeed!

Sandalwood Art

Men and boys carve magnificent sandalwood figures of Balinese dancers, elongated in the classic postures, detailed down to the long fingernails. Sandalwood fish are carved, delicate depictions of the tropical fish that lie offshore.

Dances and Shadow Plays

The Balinese town of Ubud is famed for its exciting Brueghel-like paintings crowded with men, women, children, pigs, chickens, and goats, all living in a roiling stew of riotous color. These paintings are greatly prized by collectors.

The Balinese love their nightlife. In the villages kids are awake half the night watching the dances and the shadow-puppet shows. If visitors show enthusiasm villagers will practically drag them to all night performances. Beautiful young people perform dance pantomimes illustrating ancient stories, and the entire village turns out for these performances. And they are also connoisseurs of the shadow plays based on Hindu epics. Communicating by shadows is an ancient shamanistic method of telling stories. The Balinese shadow play *Wayang Kulit* is highly stylized with story nuances that all the village children know by heart but watch again and again. The shadow puppets are made from buffalo hide and skillfully cut so the shadows they cast are pure and delicate. The shadow puppet plays are sad, ribald, inspiring in their turn.

Balinese dancers at late night gathering. PHOTO: ERNEST BEYL

Nehru called Bali "The Morning of the World"

The Balinese opera is called *Ardja*. Balinese opera goers know the old stories just as westerners know Puccini's *La Boheme*, and find no need to follow the supertitles to understand Rodolfo's love of Mimi. To watch a Balinese opera drama is to participate in Balinese life. Everyone attends. It's the sitcom of Bali.

On the Island of Bali it can be said truly—art is a way of life. The Balinese embrace art in a natural, un-self conscious way, and, in turn, their art embraces them.

The late Indian Prime Minister Jawaharal Nehru found the magnificent island an endless source of joy. He once referred to Bali as "The morning of the world."

CHAPTER SIXTEEN

LEI YUE MUN:
AN ADVENTURE IN HONG KONG DINING

When Hong Kong was a British Crown Colony, I spent a lot of time there. I was the U.S. publicist for Cathay Pacific Airways, Hong Kong & Shanghai Hotels, and even the Hong Kong Government itself. I suppose I fancied myself as a quasi-diplomat but that's another tale for another time. This tale is of dining out in Hong Kong in those days when dining was—and still is—about as good as it gets.

When I was a regular visitor, there was a tiny fishing village on the Lei Yue Mun channel, a narrow passage several hundred yards across, between the Kowloon mainland and Hong Kong Island. The village was on the Kowloon side of the harbor and villagers sold their catch commercially and also displayed all manner of sea creatures in tanks and holding pens for anyone hungry who happened by. The village was not then widely known and it was high adventure to visit it with a group of friends, purchase live seafood from the fishermen and take it to one of two or three simple restaurants there and have the cooks prepare it. There was no real menu in those Lei Yue Mun restaurants. You turned your purchases over to the cook who had only rice, onions, garlic, chilies and various greens in his crude kitchen.

On hot nights we sat outdoors beneath the stars and beneath the big jets taking off and landing at Kai Tak Airport, at that time the international airport for Hong Kong. The Lei Yue Mun fishing village was directly below the airport flight line.

It was separated from Kowloon by fast moving, shallow water from the South China Sea, and at low tide by mud and silt. There was a small ferryboat that putt-putted from a pier near the airport and on around to the channel side of the village where it landed at a rickety dock. And that was the way my Chinese and British friends and I occasionally got to Lei Yue Mun village to eat incredible seafood dinners and consume a lot of beer. But I'm ahead of my story.

Laundry at the Peninsula

Before noon one day I was sitting in the Lobby of the famed Peninsula Hotel having coffee when an American travel writer I knew walked into the hotel attended by a group of teenaged, uniformed Peninsula bellmen. They were dragging his luggage, a Louis Vuitton collection, properly scuffed and well stickered.

I invited him to join me for coffee which he did after he signed in at the front desk with a fine journalistic flourish.

He had just arrived from Bali and now he was in Hong Kong for a few days of R&R before flying back to the States. "I have to pick up my laundry here. I bring my shirts over just to get them done here at the Pen." Yes he talked like that.

Well one thing led to another and soon we had agreed to get a group together and go out somewhere to dinner that night. I suggested Lei Yue Mun.

My friend frowned but gamed it through saying that it was probably the only restaurant in Hong Kong he hadn't tried. I could see he wasn't aware of Lei Yue Mun and explained about the fishing village, and like a good reporter, he smelled a story.

That evening eight of us, led by the travel writer who was now in charge of our group, engaged two of the Peninsula's green Rolls Royce limos with their liveried drivers who drove us to the Lei Yue Mun putt-putt which then ferried us out for a Dutch treat dinner. There were three Chinese civil servants and their girlfriends, the travel writer, and me, the budding diplomat.

Off to Lei Yue Mun

For the occasion the travel writer wore a crinkly, silver plastic jumpsuit. It was a memento from some first class inaugural flight on Singapore Airlines, and he wore handmade tan leather Jodhpur boots. A Lufthansa flight bag slung over his shoulder completed the ensemble. So off we went into the hot night.

Soon the eight of us were jammed onto the small sputtering ferry-boat. We sat on wooden benches that ran along the sides of the craft with village fishermen and their families returning home with their purchases after a day in the big city—electric rice cookers, rubber boots, and big cloth bags of rice.

In a few minutes we stepped ashore on wooden duckboards that kept us above the muddy water and into a scene of frenzy. There was a din of merchant-fishermen hawking live seafood. One man held aloft a huge spiny lobster. Another pointed to very active large blue crabs scuttling around in a concrete tank. There was an enormous plastic basin filled with squirming something-or-others—huge and slimy geo-ducks, I found out later. Despite their reputed aphrodisiac qualities, we passed.

The travel writer whipped out his camera and slung it around his neck. His tape recorder dangled from a wrist cord. He was using both hands and directing an old man to stand in front a large glass tank full of small swarming fish. He used the word "smile" and pointed to his own face to indicate what he wanted. The man with the lobster came over to get in the picture.

The travel writer got the photo and held his tape recorder forward.

How much for the lobster? One of the young Chinese women with us translated. "A lot," was the answer. Fresh seafood wasn't then and isn't now inexpensive in Hong Kong—or most anywhere else.

The Mother of all Garoupas

The travel writer led our party from stall to stall and we purchased live crabs, a bucketful of shrimp, clams, sea scallops, and periwinkles to ferret out of their tiny shells with small straight pins and slurp down. No geoducks.

Then came the episode of the mother of all garoupas. And in succeeding references this fish certainly deserves an honorific capitalization.

The travel writer led us to a series of very large glass tanks in which many disconsolate fish were swimming aimlessly. He was looking for the centerpiece for our dinner. And then he found it. In one tank, almost stationary, its fins lazily fanning back and forth, was the Mother of

At Hong Kong's Lei Yue Mun, your garoupa is in a tank. PHOTO: ERNEST BEYL

all Garoupas—a huge, fat, nuclear submarine of a Garoupa, more than a yard in length, with a girth like the U.S.S. Trident, or perhaps like a middle linebacker. Its eyes were the size of small saucers, its mouth like a shovel scoop.

We wanted this Garoupa. No, we needed this Garoupa, said our leader. No other Garoupa would do. This particular Garoupa would crown our meal. It would be a Garoupa worth remembering—memorialized in print on the pages of the travel writer's important newspaper. The article would be accompanied by a photo of the travel writer himself holding up the beast. But alas, this was not to be.

The Garoupa was not Pleased

Let's get the Mother of all Garoupas out of this tank so we can really see her. The merchant demurred. The travel writer insisted. The merchant shook his head back and forth emphatically. The travel writer nodded his head up and down just as emphatically. And so it came to pass. A very large net on a long handle was brought forth. Have you ever attempted to net a fish? Even a small fish?

Several minutes later, after much splashing, heaving and grunting, the Mother was brought forth. She weighed in at 27 kilos, about 60 pounds, shaking and tossing at one end of a hand-held balancing scale. The Mother of all Garoupas was agitated. It took two men to hold the scale aloft by its rope. A crowd had gathered. It seemed like most of the village came to watch and cheer. Now the action happened very fast, like a jerky, old-time movie.

The Travel Writer was not Pleased

Beaming with pride of the chase, the travel writer asked "How much?" "Three hundred and fifty dollars U.S.," our translator replied.

By now the cheering had stopped. The onlookers smiled. The merchant frowned. The wind was out of our sails. And the Mother of all Garoupas was returned to her tank where she sulked. We settled for a junior grade, miniature submarine, took it and the rest of our purchases to one of Lei Yue Mun's restaurants and had a memorable meal anyway.

I ran into the travel writer the next afternoon in the Peninsula Lobby. He was checking out and heading for the airport. He wore his silver plastic jumpsuit. He was a fine travel writer but if he wrote about leading an assault on Lei Yue Mun I never saw the article.

CHAPTER SEVENTEEN

WHAT EVER HAPPENED TO JIM THOMPSON

I wonder what ever happened to Jim Thompson. A visit to Bangkok is not really complete for me without a visit to his house on the *klong*.

Bangkok can be exasperating and bewildering—bumper-to-bumper traffic, cloying heat, humidity. It can also be surprising and enchanting. But if you feel you may soon develop a tic in the corner of your good eye, go to Jim Thompson's house on the *klong*. You will never forget it. The house is just like Jim Thompson left it. But let me get on with the story.

Jim Thompson and Thai Silk

Jim Thompson was an American architect who enlisted in the U.S. Army in 1940. He was assigned to the Office of Strategic Services, all hush-hush, and was sent to Asia. He was scheduled to parachute into Thailand to assist with the liberation of the country when World War II ended. Later he came to love Thailand and returned there and made it his home.

Thompson had an artistic eye. He became interested in the almost dormant cottage industry of producing Thai silk, a lustrous, handwoven fabric that had long since been replaced by cheap, machine-made goods. Thompson led the move to revive the Thai silk industry. He organized the worker-artisans and championed the results of their work.

The King and I and Thai Silk

When he was convinced of its quality he gathered samples of the best and most beautiful Thai silk and journeyed to New York City to create a stir with the beautiful fabrics. Thai Silk (now with a capital S) soon became a high fashion, luxury product. In 1951 when Richard Rodgers and Oscar Hammerstein made the Broadway musical "The King and I" starring Yul Brynner and Gertrude Lawrence, the costumes were hand-stitched Thai Silk. They were gorgeous. Thai Silk acquired the world-wide reputation it has today.

Jim Thompson's House on the Klong

Later, back in Bangkok, Jim Thompson purchased six weathered, peak-roofed, native teak, country houses. He moved them to the *Maha Nag Klong* (canal) and there joined them together. Thompson lived in this simple but elegant dwelling, which he turned into a house museum, a showplace for his striking collection of valuable Asian art. It is still there. But Jim Thompson isn't. He vanished over the Easter weekend in 1967 while on a holiday with friends in the Malaysian Cameron Highlands. There was no trace of him ever.

The Jim Thompson Mystery

What ever happened to Jim Thompson? Well, some said he was done in by jealous nationalists who felt he was exploiting the Thai silk weavers. Others said he ran afoul of elements that believed he sacked the country for precious Siamese artifacts and hid them away in his house. Still others postulated that Thompson's wartime U.S. Army OSS contacts and experiences made him a marked man in Southeast Asia. Finally, one opinion, and a likely one in my view, was that when out for an afternoon walk he fell into a poacher's pit trap, was injured, and to cover their tracks, the poachers did him in. Some said a tiger ate him.

Although an international search was mounted for Jim Thompson, complete with private detectives, government analysts, and mystical, metaphysical seers, no trace of him was ever found.

But whenever I listen to the magnificent music from "The King and I" or watch the movie with Yul Brynner and the incredibly beautiful Deborah Kerr, I think of Jim Thompson, and I think of his house on the *klong*, where I might like to live out my days wearing a Thai Silk robe.

CHAPTER EIGHTEEN

MONGKOK AND THE SNAKE SHOP

In those days—the 1980s—I was visiting Hong Kong a lot. It was during the run-up to the British handover of their Crown Colony to the People's Republic of China and I was doing some PR work for His Majesty's Service. I got to know Hong Kong pretty well, had friends there among the expats and the Chinese who worked for them.

Back in San Francisco I purchased an Apple 2E for my six-year-old daughter Laurel when they first came out in 1983. Her first grade class was learning how to operate computers and she soaked it up on the Apple with games in which rabbits jumped from one place to another. If Laurel managed to maneuver the rabbit into its hole the computer gave a satisfying "ping, ping." As fast as I could buy kids' computer programs, Laurel figured them out and lost interest in a few days.

Now back in Hong Kong there was a multi-story building in Kowloon where I could pick up pirated programs for a few dollars each. So one day I went out to the Mongkok district to increase Laurel's stock of computer rabbits and other animals. And that's how I came to drink the elixir of a snake's gall bladder.

The Mongkok Snake Shop

Mongkok is one of the most populous of the world's urban spaces. Residents live there as close together as mahjongg tiles. It's a teeming neighborhood within Kowloon (itself a teeming city), within the larger teeming city of Hong Kong. One morning I took the Kowloon subway to Mongkok. I was in quest of bootleg computer software for Laurel. I easily located the large arcade where it was sold but it was not due to open for another hour. I decided to wander around the crowded neighborhood. As I turned a corner I came upon a large crowd in front of a street-level shop. The crowd pushed forward. I joined it. Soon I

Hong Kong snake shop. PHOTO: ERNEST BEYL

was close enough to see a white-coated man remove a long slithering snake from a wire basket. I was standing in front of a snake shop. Nothing unusual about that in Hong Kong; there were many snake shops that catered to the Chinese who made soup of the slithering serpents. And nothing unusual about eating snakes either; the Chinese have always had a taste for the exotic beast. They have always enjoyed not only snake, but dog meat, camel hump, civet cat, and even bear paws. I have eaten snake soup and dog meat, but not camel hump or bear paws.

The Healthful Elixir

While I stood there in the crowd in front of the snake shop, a white-coated technician—an alchemist perhaps—swung the snake in a fast frantic arc and dispatched it with a bang to its head against the curbstone. Then, as I watched spellbound—pirate software forgotten— he slit open the snake, extracted a small organ and squeezed a tiny bit of black liquid from it into a small glass. And, to my fascination, individuals in the crowd pushed forward, paid the alchemist a few Hong Kong dollars and did "bottoms up"—drinking down this healthful elixir from the snake's gall bladder.

And, one after another, the hapless snakes bit the concrete, giving their gall bladders for health and science.

Bottoms Up

"Okay," I said to myself, "this is what you must do in Hong Kong. I will hate myself later if I don't do this." Yes, I shoved some Hong Kong dollars into the hand of an assistant, watched as the alchemist smacked my snake on the curb, slit it open, took out its gall bladder and squeezed its liquid into a glass. I grabbed the glass and tossed down the contents.

Bitter as lost love! But I had a zeal that knew no bounds. I was buoyed with self-worth. I felt like I had conquered Genghis Khan. I threw my shoulders back, turned, walked back to software arcade and bought Laurel several computer games.

Later, back in the Peninsula Hotel lobby, I ordered a coffee and was happy with myself. Soon I was joined at my table by a Chinese man I knew from the Hong Kong Tourist Association. I could hardly wait to tell him about my exciting morning.

I did and then asked, "Why do they drink that stuff?" My friend looked at me for a moment and then told me that the liquid from a snake's gall bladder was a tonic. "Good for your manhood," he said.

CHAPTER NINETEEN

Goanese sailors painting the side of a P&O passenger ship. PHOTO: ERNEST BEYL

PORT OUT, STARBOARD HOME WITH THE P&O: FIJI TO SAN FRANCISCO ABOARD S. S. HIMALAYA

Have you ever wondered how the word "posh"—meaning high quality or elegant service—came into being? In 1837 the first steamships of the P&O—Peninsular and Oriental Steam Navigation Company—began service from England to India. This was before the opening of the Suez Canal and P&O passengers traveled overland from the Mediterranean, across the desert by camel to the Red Sea where they transferred to another waiting company steamship. As a courtesy, dignitaries were assigned the cooler cabins on the shady side—or port side—of the vessel going out to India. And they were assigned the shady side—starboard—going home from India to England. Their tickets were accordingly stamped P.O.S.H.—Port Out, Starboard Home.

Steamship Himalaya

In the early 1950s, I got a job as press officer on P&O's steamship Himalaya. She was a 28,000-ton passenger ship and at the time I sailed aboard her carried about 1,000 passengers and a crew of 500. The ship was launched in 1948 in her home port of London, and was finally withdrawn from service and scrapped in1974. Himalaya was a fine ship. Even today, when I see huge cruise ships in the bay looking like misshapen ice cube trays lying on their side, I miss the old P&O steamship. She looked like a ship should look: She had a single funnel amidships; she was not air-conditioned (I don't think any passenger ships of that vintage were); and she had ceiling fans that whirled slowly in some of the public rooms. There was a great charm and gentility about sailing aboard these handsome old vessels.

Press Officer Duties

So what did a press officer do aboard those P&O passenger ships? My job was to turn out a daily news-sheet for the passengers. News came in by clattering telex from the BBC in London. I digested it into short, one paragraph bites, and printed it on a cranky mimeograph machine called a Roneo that spit out copies in bright purple ink. My other job aboard Himalaya was to hang out with newsworthy passengers, write news releases about them, and later encourage local press to interview them while we were in port.

The job was not unpleasant and it was not particularly taxing.

Pink Gin on the Verandah

To join Himalaya I flew from San Francisco to Suva in the Fijian Islands. It was a long flight on Qantas and I arrived exhausted, and holed-up in my hotel room for a couple of days before the ship arrived. As required, I stopped by the P&O shipping agents' office to announce my readiness for the upcoming voyage. I met a portly "Brit" who looked like actor Sydney Greenstreet and wore a stained and rumpled white linen suit and a Panama hat. Early that afternoon he took me to his club—a one story, tin roofed shed. We sat on the verandah and sipped pink gin. At four o'clock the rains came, as they always do in the tropics, and beat noisily on the tin roof.

The Captain and His Lava Lava

The next morning as I looked out the window of my hotel room I saw S.S. Himalaya riding at anchor. After lunch I took a small launch out to the ship and walked up the gangway. As I boarded, a tall figure in a crisp white uniform met me. He was the starchy Staff Captain and he was waiting for me. Seems I was expected earlier. That was the first P&O lesson I learned—always get up early, and then show up early. The Staff Captain marched me up several decks to meet Captain Latham in his cabin just off the bridge. A youngish man of about 50, salt and pepper hair, medium height, greeted me. He was stripped to the waist and wearing a lava lava—a man's ankle-length sarong—wrapped around his middle, with one end twisted into a knot and shoved southward. Lava lavas are known all over the South Pacific, but I had expected a formal captain with white, sharply creased pants and shiny brass buttons dotting a starched jacket.

By the third day at sea Captain Latham and I had become buddies. When he realized I approved of his lava lava, he gave me one with great ceremony.

A Polyglot Crew

Himalaya's route to the point I joined her was Sydney, Auckland, and Suva. Then with me aboard we sailed for Honolulu, Vancouver, and San Francisco. The weather was calm and fair. The ocean was blue and smooth.

Crew aboard Himalaya was a polyglot bunch. Officers were all Englishmen, as were the cabin stewards. I had a tiny cabin with one porthole and an adjoining cabin which I used as my office. A Cockney named Oakes was my cabin steward. Every afternoon he brought tea, then drew me a bath in a tiny closet down the companionway. When I returned to my cabin, Oakes had laid out my required costume for cocktails and dinner. Two or three times a week it was formal wear—my ratty tuxedo.

The engine room crewmembers were Pakistani and wore full, henna-dyed, beards. Dining room stewards and kitchen workers were from the state of Goa in southwestern India, once a Portuguese colony. One Goanese was the curry cook. That's all he did. He ground his own curry powder and with it prepared blazing hot dishes that I came to love.

A Lava Lava Memory

And so it went. I turned out the Himalaya news-sheet, I interviewed passengers, drank pink gins—which I had taken a fancy to—and I ate blazing curry. During off hours I hung out with Captain Latham in his cabin, or in the officers's wardroom. We both wore our lava lavas. Then, one morning I looked out my porthole just as we were passing under the Golden Gate Bridge. My adventure aboard the grand old Himalaya was over.

I still wear my lava lava occasionally. Stripped to the waist, I wear it around the house when my wife is out—but I refrain from wearing it to Gino and Carlo or Original Joe's.

CHAPTER TWENTY

TRAVELING AND THE LIFE OF A SERIOUS EATER

Traveling and dining often combine to enhance the total experience. Perhaps you have noticed this also, but somehow food always seems to taste better when you're on the road. And, dining while traveling provides wonderful subject matter for the traveler's note book. Here are some dining notes I found recently and polished a bit for this chapter. But these dining recollections from a few early notebooks do not concern themselves with gastronomic super galaxies I experienced along the way.

Anyone who is anybody has written about Chez Panisse, the French Laundry, Le Cirque, Spago, El Bulli, Taillevent, and other such star-marked (or crossed) temples of gastronomy. Big time—or small time—restaurant reviewers yap, yelp, and yammer, with cool critiques. Let's call that syndrome "Big moments in the life of a major league gourmand." I'm susceptible too. I admit it. Isn't it grand to be grand with grand cuisine? But let me turn the page and give you some big moments in the life of a major league eater who has enjoyed dining off-the-track—call them memorable stops along the way.

Here then are a few personal dining experiences recalled over many years. Forget the stars, the toques, the forks or what have you. You just might want to give these a checkmark in your restaurant notebook.

Dozier's Barbecue

Years ago my brother-in-law, whom I had never met, lived in Houston. Shortly after my wife and I married, her sister invited the newlyweds down there for a few days so they could kick the tires and check me out. I apparently hit it off as a new relative and each day brother-in-law Max chose a new restaurant to take us to lunch or dinner. "You San Francisco types will be surprised at the great food we have down here," he said. So, for almost a week we ate in French, Italian, Chinese and other assorted restaurants. They were all okay—nothing to get excited about—but Joan and I praised them anyway. Then, when we had one more day in Texas, Max ran dry. He couldn't come up with a place he thought would please us. We sat on the patio having a beer when his wife Joyce had an idea. "Well," she started, "I've wanted to mention this all week but Max nixed it." Then, turning to him she asked "Why don't we go to your brother's place in Fulshear?"

"They wouldn't like it," Max replied.

"Sure we would," I said, being a good house guest. "What's your brother's place?"

"Barbecue," Joyce answered. Max was silent. "Dozier's Barbecue. You might like it. It's not fancy, but it's good." An inspired choice!

Opened in 1957 Dozier's Barbecue was at a rural crossroad in a tiny town named Fulshear. It had a gas pump, some picnic tables and a smokehouse. Max's brother fixed us up with some ribs, smoked with his signature pecan wood. It was sensational. Even today, when I think about barbecue—and I do often—I think about Dozier's. It's still there.

Cathay Pacific Airways

I was fortunate enough to fly Cathay Pacific Airways, First Class, from Hong Kong to San Francisco back in the sixties. The Boeing 747 left Hong Kong in the evening. After a good meal with a French vintage burgundy and a movie, I fell asleep. In the middle of that short night flying east over the Pacific, I awakened and turned on my overhead light. In a moment the flight attendant, an elegant young Chinese woman with a stylish asymmetrical hair-do, was at my side.

"I see you are awake, Sir. Are you hungry?" I was. "How would you like a nice bowl of wonton noodle soup?" I would.

She set up my tray table with a dragon embroidered placemat, a porcelain chopstick holder with beautifully-carved wooden chopsticks, a curved porcelain spoon, and a small saucer holding a few green chilies into which she poured a bit of soy sauce. Fifteen minutes later my sky angel reappeared with a large, blue and white Chinese bowl. It steamed with a rich broth in which swam a mountain of tiny noodles, thin-skinned, shrimp-filled wontons, bits of chicken and a few chopped scallions.

I tucked a linen napkin into my open collar and slurped my soup. It was magnificent. Then I turned out the overhead light and slept like a baby.

Nepenthe

At least once a year since the early fifties I make a pilgrimage down California's Highway 1 to Big Sur for an afternoon at Nepenthe, the iconic restaurant perched more than 800 feet high on a bluff above the Pacific. Nepenthe is synonymous with Big Sur and the laid back, bohemian lifestyle.

There, I discharge my batteries. I say "discharge" because my batteries are usually overcharged. I like to detach all the wires, sit on Nepenthe's terrace, look south to the Santa Lucia mountains on the left and the Pacific Ocean on the right, and sip a Bloody Mary. Then—always following the same routine—I order an Ambrosia Burger. And that does it for me.

The name Nepenthe derives from the Greek meaning "forgetfulness of sorrow." I like that. I'm an optimistic guy and avoid sorrow like I avoid poison oak.

Nepenthe's origins go back to the 1920s when a homesteader built a small log cabin on that bluff. Later, Orson Welles bought it, intending to spend his honeymoon there with bride Rita Hayworth. However, the famous pair never honeymooned there. In fact, no one remembers them ever coming to the Big Sur property. Bill and Lolly Fassett purchased the Welles-Hayworth cabin in 1947 and two years later opened Nepenthe on what may be the most glorious meeting of land and ocean on this planet. Members of the Fassett family still own it.

Over those many years Henry Miller, Richard Burton, Elizabeth Taylor, Salvador Dali, Jack Kerouac, and thousands of tourists and hippies have all stopped at Nepenthe to dream, meditate and celebrate. In 1965 Mararishi Mahesh Yogi was carried across the Nepenthe terrace on a platform covered with flowers. When I go there to discharge my batteries, a platform with flowers isn't necessary.

Nepenthe (Big Sur). PHOTO: FRED LYON

Durgin Park

On the second floor in Boston's old Faneuil Hall, an ancient marketplace near the city's waterfront, is a 180-year-old restaurant named Durgin Park. Many years ago I went there for lunch, sat at one of the communal tables and ordered rare roast beef. "Bone-in Yankee Cut," the waitress asked me? Absolutely! I was a skinny youngster then. A few minutes later a guy with a pony tail and a three-day beard sat down across from me. After a few more minutes the waitress returned with an enormous hunk of magnificent rare roast beef for me. My table mate looked at my plate and said "Roast Beef."

Now, I don't really know what went wrong. Maybe she didn't like the guy, but she returned after a bit with his order—a thinly sliced mound of okay roast beef and a few vegetables.

"I want what he's having," he said pointing to my plate.

"He's having the Yankee Cut. You're having the Poor Man's Roast Beef," She said.

"Bring me one."

"I can't take that back now," she said pointing to his plate.

"Just leave it here."

He ate the Poor Man's Roast Reef and then he ate the Yankee Cut.

By that time I was on my Indian Pudding—corn meal and black molasses—with vanilla ice cream.

"And, I'll have one of those too," he said next time the waitress came by. And he did.

Harry's Café de Wheels

The meat pie is to Australians what the hamburger is to Americans. More than 30 years ago on a vacation in Sydney I discovered the joys of the meat pie at Harry's Café de Wheels. Before writing this at 10:45 this morning I made a call to David Ellis, a writer friend in Sydney, and woke him up at 3:45 tomorrow morning his time. I wanted to know if Harry's Café de Wheels was still there. "Well, it was yesterday when I went there for a pie," David replied sourly.

I'm glad of that because Harry's Café de Wheels is a Sydney institution—a pale pea-green food stand set up in a small caravan, or house trailer as we would call it. A sign on the caravan reads "We Serve Snappy Snacks." What Harry's serves are pies with peas. Hot meat pies with a large spoonful of cooked peas plopped on the golden brown crust. A squirt of catsup tops it off. Harry's sits next to the Woolloomooloo navy docks in Sydney and is open most of the night. Sailors and other revelers from nearby King's Cross drop by for pies and peas. I did! The iconic food stand opened in 1938 and is included on the New South Wales National Trust Register.

Sir Scott's Oasis

The best steak I ever had was not in a New York or Chicago steakhouse as one might expect, but in Montana where I go fly fishing each year. My buddy and fishing guide Vince Gordon takes me to Sir Scott's Oasis in Manhattan, Montana after a day on the Yellowstone or Madison rivers. We like to re-live the day's catch-and-release fly fishing over a steak dinner.

Manhattan is a small farming community of about 1500 residents. The Oasis is Manhattan's superstar restaurant and steak fans come from all over the Gallatin Valley in southeast Montana to dig in. In fact, they come from all over the country to try those sensational steaks.

The restaurant originally opened in the 1960s. Scott Westphal, who began working for the former owner when he was 16, took it over in 1980. Scott serves only aged USDA prime and choice beef. It's corn-fed "finished" in Greeley, Colorado and shipped to Manhattan—remember, that's Manhattan, Montana.

CHAPTER TWENTY-ONE

DINING WITH THE DOCTOR IN SINGAPORE

One of my food writer idols, Calvin Trillin, said, "Health food makes me sick."

But let's get on with this journalistic, public service. I once went to dinner in a Singapore restaurant that featured a doctor instead of a maître d'—white jacket, thermometer, stethoscope, grave expression. The whole works.

Before leading me to my table the doctor took my temperature, my pulse, my blood pressure, listened to the rumblings in my chest, felt to see if I was sweaty (I was), pressed the fleshy parts of both hands, and began talking to me about the humours.

My Humours were out of Balance

You know about the humours don't you? Air, fire, and water. The act, or art, of breathing, feeling too warm or too cold, with lots of bodily fluids sloshing around. My Singapore doctor-maître d' ruled that my humours were out of balance. And I suppose they were. I had just flown nearly 24 hours to get to Singapore and since my arrival had been in and out of super air-conditioned rooms and taxis and had now met my companion from the Singapore Government Tourist Office who said I didn't look well and that she had just the thing—dinner in a newly fashionable restaurant, in short—dining with the doctor.

I was Queasy

At the conclusion of the consultation the doctor-maître d' wrote out a prescription for my dinner and an assistant led us to a table. I was queasy before the food arrived. I ate a few bites of this and that. Something sweet to strengthen my tissue. Something sour to stimulate the digestion. Something salty to cleanse obstructions, and something pungent

A street fortune teller in Singapore. PHOTO: ERNEST BEYL

to purify the blood. During the Tang Dynasty there was a renowned doctor, Sun Simiao, who believed in the curative powers of food. Why argue? He lived to be 101.

When I got back to the hotel I took two aspirin, an Imodium tablet, quaffed down some restorative Alka Seltzer, hit the sack and slept peacefully. My humours were balanced. That was a long time ago, thousands of Chinese meals ago.

CHAPTER TWENTY-TWO

ANTONIO'S EMBARRASSMENT: MATADOR ORDONEZ IN MEXICO

On Monday, November 19, 1962 there appeared in the *New York Times* a brief story about a multimillionaire named Antonio Ordonez. The story read:

Spain's top matador 30-year-old Antonio Ordonez announced his retirement after a bullfight today. Considered one of the greatest matadors in history, Ordonez was gored in August 1961 after completing most of the 40 fights scheduled that season under a reported 15,000,000-peseta (about $252,000) contract.

A spectacular fighter, he earned as much as 750,000 pesetas (about $12,320) for one fight in Madrid.

Ordonez was tossed by a bull and twice badly gored in the right thigh during a bullfight at Salamanca in northern Spain in September.

It was the second serious accident of the season for the handsome bullfighter. Last April he was badly gored—also in the right thigh—in Mexico and spent three weeks in the hospital.

Ordonez is the son of the late Cayetano Ordonez, also a famous Spanish bullfighter.

One Sunday Afternoon

But now let me tell you about one Sunday afternoon in Mexico—the afternoon that Antonio Ordonez was gored and embarrassed by an angry and erratic bull.

Plaza Monumental, The Bullring by the Sea, sits like an inverted concrete teacup a few hundred yards from the Pacific near the Mexican border town, Tijuana. The Sunday afternoon of April 29, 1962 the plaza was occupied by 23,000 bullfight aficionados, many of them sitting in the arena's aisles or jammed together at the bullring's entrance.

Numero Uno

They had come to see Antonio Ordonez, *numero uno*, usually billed as the world's greatest matador. They had paid from $3.50 to $11.50 for a seat to watch the chunky young man—who had been gored 18 times in 14 years—kill two bulls from the Xajay Ranch.

It was to be his first appearance in Tijuana. The fact that Ernest Hemingway had written about Ordonez two years earlier in *Life* magazine, and the fact that Tijuana is easily accessible to bullfight fans and the merely curious, drew the crowd—the largest in Tijuana's bullfight history.

Spectators—including this writer—were jocular but intent. This was not just another border-town bullfight of questionable appeal. It was one of the great bullfighting events. There was a crackle of excitement such as experienced at opening day of the World Series. Spectators knew they were going to see something worth watching. *Numero Uno* was going to perform—the young Spaniard who risked his life every Sunday afternoon.

Slow and Superbly Graceful Passes

Jesus Cordoba, an agile Mexican who was senior matador that day, fought the first bull. He fought it no better or no worse than I had seen on many Sunday afternoons in Tijuana or elsewhere in Mexico. But it did not matter, for who was really there to watch Cordoba? The crowd was buying beer, smoking, people-watching, squirming in anticipation of seeing Antonio Ordonez create something graceful, dangerous, and beautiful to watch.

Early in every bullfight there takes place a series of cape passes known as the *quite* (key-tay)—literally meaning to take away. It is the taking away of the bull from a terrain in the ring where he has caused danger. Usually it refers to a series of passes planned to distract the bull from the picador's horse, and to lead him through a series of short, fierce charges across the ring to the second mounted picador. The task of picadors is to plunge a sharp lance into the bull's neck muscle to cause the bull to lower his head.

Participating matadors take their turns passing the bull in rotation and it is during the *quite* that spectators have the opportunity to com-

Spanish matador Antonio Ordonez, fighting off his handlers after he was gored.
PHOTO: ERNEST BEYL

pare one matador's style with another. It was during the *quite* of Cordoba's first bull that Ordonez stepped into the ring and made his first slow and superbly graceful pass of the afternoon—the bull's horns coming within inches of the man on each pass.

Man and Bull had Fused

There is a quality found in champions of all sports—and indeed in performing artists of all types—that is difficult to describe. Call it a smooth deliberateness. Or call it an unconscious, throwaway of style, as though style did not really matter at all. Ordonez passing that bull closely gave one the peculiar feeling that for a split second man and bull had fused into a motionless moment of grace and beauty. Then, in the next split second man and bull moved smoothly, quietly, and without frills.

The Bull Hooked a Horn into the Matador's Thigh

Cordoba killed his bull. When the trumpet blew its signal for the entrance of the second bull it was so quiet in Plaza Monumental I thought I could hear beer foaming in the paper cups. Then Ordonez was in the ring performing those incredibly graceful passes—*veronicas* in this case. Already the crowd was rewarding him with *oles*. But a scant five minutes later the 30-year-old multi millionaire matador was in pain—surprised, shocked, angry, and perhaps even embarrassed.

It happened during the *faena*—the third and last portion of the formal bullfight when the matador passes the bull with a small, heart-shaped red cloth called a *muleta*. Suddenly the bull turned and hooked a horn into the matador's right thigh. Blood began trickling down the tight embroidered black pants he wore and staining the sand of the ring as the bull was diverted by someone in Ordonez's *cuadrilla*—group of ring assistants. Ordonez refused to be led or carried from the ring to the infirmary.

Ordonez Killed the Bull

He fought off his concerned well-wishers and handlers who entered the ring. He kicked off his black slippers and snaked out of his jacket. Knowing that he must, in his pink stockings he limped back to the bull. The crowd sat in silence and watched as the man, who was leaving puddles of his blood in the sand, moved carefully through the remaining *muleta* passes before he felt he could safely kill this bull whose lethal qualities had just been demonstrated. Then Ordonez killed his bull—unaided. He then allowed himself to be assisted from the ring.

Antonio Ordonez received $15,000 for his work that afternoon. It's a tough way to make a living.

These few paragraphs about one Sunday afternoon in Tijuana, Mexico are not meant to be either defense of, or a diatribe against bullfighting. They are intended only to relate an incident—an indefensible incident perhaps, but one of drama, surprise, shock, pain, blood, and considerable beauty.

Novelist Ernest Hemingway was a bullfight aficionado. He not only wrote about the *corrida* in *Death in the Afternoon*, but many years later wrote a book called *The Dangerous Summer*, in which he told of following two matadors—Luis Miguel Dominguin, and Antonio Ordonez—as they fought bulls in the summer of 1959, *mano a mano* (in competition with each other).

CHAPTER TWENTY-THREE

ANGEL FALLS

Naively I thought I would take the photographer, the video camera-man, and the models right up to the foot of Angel Falls, let them get a little spray in their faces—to add a note of realism—and then shoot what I needed for the cruise line promotion. I hadn't done my home-work.

My idea was to charter a DC-3 in Porto Ordaz, located in Venezuela where the Orinoco River meets a tributary called the Caroni, then fly over the Venezuelan jungle to somewhere—I didn't know where—get out of the DC-3 at some deserted airstrip, arrange the models—two good-looking women within the cruise line's demographics—and two handsome and rugged linebacker types—place them strategically—looking up at the 3,287-foot, vertical drop of Angel Falls, the highest waterfall, with the longest drop, in the world.

The House of the Gods

Well, eventually I did charter the DC-3. When I asked the pilot how old the airplane was, he said "very old," and pointed to a small brass plaque on the instrument panel. It read *Servivensa 1949*. Photographer, cameraman, my four models, and I piled in and we flew to Angel Falls. That is we flew around the *Auyantepui*, the table-top *tepui* ("house of the gods") from which Angel Falls issues. We gazed nervously through the opening where the copilot had removed the airplane's door so the photographer and the cameraman could shoot easily. It was spectac-ular—an unbelievably long white column of water. The elevation of our airplane was several hundred feet below the *tepui's* summit and we looked up from the open door to the flat surface at the *tepui's* top, then gazed the long way down into clouds of mist as the falls churned into the mesa below.

Angel Falls in Venezuela. PHOTO: FLICKR.COM/ ENT108

These *tepuis* in Venezuela's Canaima National Park are composed of sheer blocks of sandstone that rise from the jungle below. They are what remain of an ancient plateau. Over eons the plateau eroded and the flat-topped *tepuis* rose dramatically into the sky.

Daredevil Pilot Jimmie Angel

Angel Falls is named for Jimmie Angel, a daredevil pilot and explorer, who flew a small aircraft over *Auyantepui* in 1933 looking for a valuable ore bed. The huge waterfall was not well-known outside of Venezuela at the time. Five years later he returned in a Flamingo monoplane. He intended to land on top of the *tepui* to scout mining sites, but crash-landed and nosedived into the soft ground. He righted the craft with the help of his wife and two passengers, but takeoff was impossible. They abandoned the airplane, and over 11 days the party made its tortuous way off the *tepui* and to the nearest settlement.

His Ashes were scattered over Angel Falls

Jimmie Angel's airplane remained on top of *Auyantepui* until 1970. It was then disassembled and brought down by military helicopters.

Now it's an attraction at the airport terminal in Cuidad Bolivar. Jimmie Angel suffered a head injury in 1956 attempting to land an airplane in Panama and within a few months he died. His ashes were scattered over Angel Falls in 1960.

CHAPTER TWENTY-FOUR

"I HAVE LAID ASIDE BUSINESS AND GONE A' FISHING."

Many years ago I had a casual friendship in Sun Valley with author Ernest Hemingway. It occurred because we both loved fly fishing. The next few chapters are about my short friendship with Hemingway, my admiration for him as a writer, and about our shared passion.

There is a long and rich history of essayists, novelists, short story writers, and amateur scribblers who have written about the art of fishing. It dates back to 1496 when Dame Juliana Berners, the prioress of St. Mary of Sopwell near St. Albans in Herfordshire, wrote *Treatise of Fishing with an Angle*. In 1662 Colonel Robert Venables wrote *The Experienced Angler*, and in 1653 Izaak Walton published his classic *The Compleat Angler*—"I have laid aside business and gone a' fishing," he wrote.

And so it went. The art of fishing (or angling)—especially fly fishing—became a proper subject for sporting literature. These days there's a lively trade in collecting valuable books and illustrated manuscripts on fishing. Somewhere in my collection is a small, pale green, leather bound volume of *Little Rivers* by Henry Van Dyke, a 19th century clergyman. *Little Rivers* is described as "A book of Essays in Profitable Idleness." I still engage in the "profitable idleness" of fly fishing.

In 1925 fisherman Ernest Hemingway published a book of short stories called *In Our Time*. It features a story called *Big Two-Hearted River*. Semi-autobiographical, the two-part story concerns young Nick Adams on a fishing excursion on Michigan's Upper Peninsula. Hemingway wrote about Nick Adams seeing trout in a pool, "He watched them, holding themselves with their noses in the current. Many trout in deep, fast moving water, slightly distorted as he watched far down through the glassy convex surface of the pool..." To my mind that brief passage captures the essence of fishing for trout. I can see those fish in the pool.

In 1926 Hemingway's first novel, *The Sun Also Rises,* was published. It caused a sensation. His story of a group of American expatriates idling in Paris, attending bullfights in Pamplona and fishing in Spain's Irati River, still resonates after all these years. I read it as a youth. I re-read it today. As a fisherman, I remember the scenes from Hemingway's chapter in which Jake Barnes (fictional counterpart of Hemingway) and his friend Bill Gorton fish for trout in the Irati River. Consider this brief passage: "I did not feel the first trout strike. When I started to pull up I felt that I had one and brought him, fighting and bending the rod almost double, out of the boiling water at the foot of the falls, and swung him up onto the dam." To me that's Hemingway at his finest.

The short essays that follow are about my appreciation of Ernest Hemingway—his stories, his incisive prose, his fishing acumen—and how he has influenced me.

CHAPTER TWENTY-FIVE

IT HAPPENED IN SUN VALLEY

The song "It Happened in Sun Valley" was written for the 1941 motion picture Sun Valley Serenade. *Lyrics were by Mack Gordon, music by Harry Warren. It was published by Twentieth Century Music Corporation. Glenn Miller and his Orchestra performed the tune.*

Sun Valley, the internationally-renowned resort in Idaho's Wood River Valley with a backdrop of the rugged Sawtooth Mountains, opened in 1936. It was the vision of W. Averell Harriman, at that time chairman of the Union Pacific Railroad. From its headquarters in Omaha, Nebraska, the Union Pacific operated passenger and freight trains across the American Northwest. A spur of the direct line touched at a small sheep town in Idaho called Shoshone. Harriman, an avid skier, reasoned that if he were able to establish a top, European-style, ski resort within a short traveling distance from Shoshone, he would gain two advantages. He would increase business for Union Pacific and he would have a place to ski.

After selecting the site for his visionary resort, Harriman contacted Steve Hannagan, the famed press agent who had successfully promoted Miami Beach, Florida, and took him to the proposed site in Idaho. It was Hannagan who named the would-be resort Sun Valley. Just as he had done with Miami Beach, Hannagan put Sun Valley "on the map." He convinced the United States Postal Service to list it as a destination for the U.S. mail. Highly influential in Hollywood, Hannagan and his corps of fellow press agents convinced the top movie stars of the day to spend their holidays on the ski slopes in Sun Valley. Clark Gable, Claudette Colbert, Gary Cooper, Lucille Ball, Erroll Flynn, Ray Milland, Paulette Goddard, and many others made the visit and were photographed skiing, tobogganing, ice skating, even swimming in a heated, outdoor pool. Actress Norma Shearer, who loved Sun Valley, even married her ski instructor.

In 1941 Sun Valley was featured in a movie. It was called *Sun Valley Serenade* and starred Norwegian figure skater and actress Sonja Henie, actor John Payne, and comic Milton Berle. Swing bandleader Glenn Miller and his orchestra were featured and played the key tune "It Happened in Sun Valley."

But it was famed author Ernest Hemingway who burnished the resort's reputation. Sun Valley had become a year-round destination known for its trout fishing and game hunting as well as for its winter sports. Hemingway, who loved skiing, fishing, and hunting, was invited to be a guest there by Hannagan's resident publicity man at the time, Gene Van Guilder. The word was passed to Hemingway, who at that time was living in Cuba. He was offered Sun Valley guests facilities at no cost for two years. In return he would be expected to cooperate modestly with the Sun Valley publicity department. At the time, the author was working on a new novel about the Spanish Civil War. He loved the western mountains for their rugged beauty and was longing to get out of the heat and humidity of Cuba. Besides, his second marriage—to Pauline Pfeiffer—was floundering. He responded to the offer saying that he may or may not show up there one day and take a look.

And one day in September 1939, without prior announcement, Hemingway turned up at Sun Valley in a dusty, black Buick convertible. With him was a beautiful woman named Martha Gellhorn who would later become his third wife. The management put the Hemingway party into a Sun Valley Lodge suite—number 206—which he later referred to as the Glamour House. It was there that the author completed his famous novel about the Spanish Civil War, *For Whom the Bell Tolls*.

CHAPTER TWENTY-SIX

Sun Valley hunting and fishing guide Taylor "Beartracks" Williams with his annotated copy of a galley proof of F*or Whom the Bell Tolls*, by Ernest Hemingway. PHOTO: AL BRACK

TAYLOR "BEARTRACKS" WILLIAMS

In the 1950s the Steve Hannagan organization—still in charge of Sun Valley publicity—offered me the job of resident publicist. I had been a newspaper reporter in San Francisco and later the PR guy for a small airline in Fort Worth, Texas. Going to Sun Valley would not only get me out of Texas, but was a dream job. And I loved skiing and fly fishing. So I took off for Idaho in the early fall of 1954. I moved into a log cabin in Ketchum with my wife and two sons.

Ketchum at that time was a small village that had begun as a Basque sheep station. Our cabin was on a tributary of the Wood River and from the back porch I could see trout swimming in a deep pool. Furthermore, it was right down the road—about two miles—from my Sun Valley office. One day after I had been on the job for several weeks, I asked Taylor "Beartracks" Williams into my office. He was the senior Sun Valley hunting and fishing guide, and a friend of Hemingway who at the time was living in Cuba. Hemingway's regard for Taylor Williams can be appreciated when you learn that the famed author had given Williams an annotated set of galley proofs of *For Whom the Bell Tolls*, a priceless gift. Later, at Williams's suggestion, Hemingway gave me an autographed first edition of *The Old Man and the Sea*. On the flyleaf he wrote "To Ernie Beyl, from Ernie Hemingway."

The meeting with "Beartracks" Williams in my office was pre-arranged and because I wanted to write a publicity story about the author-annotated copy of *For Whom the Bell Tolls*, he brought it along. That day he also brought something else as well. He was carrying a fly rod case. After we had talked about the Hemingway galley proofs and I had made a lot of notes I changed the subject and asked him what he had in the rod case. He unscrewed the cap, shook out a fly rod and assembled it—a seven-and-a-half foot, black fiberglass rod with red wrappings and a cigar-shaped cork handle. He said he had built the rod for Hemingway but the author didn't like it. It was too stiff, he felt, and besides, by that time he was into marlin fishing in the Gulf Stream. I gave Williams $25 for the rod and later used it once during the time I lived in Sun Valley.

CHAPTER TWENTY-SEVEN

Fishing with Hemingway's fly rod. PHOTO: ERNEST BEYL

FISHING WITH HEMINGWAY'S FLY ROD

The winter skiing season at Sun Valley hadn't begun. No snow yet. And I had some time on my hands. But, the fly fishing season was open. So I took the Hemingway rod (as I had come to call it) down to Silver Creek, the demanding, spring-fed trout stream near Sun Valley. In sneakers and jeans, with a box of flies I had tied myself, I parked my old station wagon near the stream and slogged through a wet meadow dodging the cow pies. When I got near Silver Creek I was almost up to my knees in black mud and as I pulled myself ahead by the reeds growing along the bank I was sucked deeper.

I finally was able to get off a couple of casts in the direction of the stream. One turned out to be a reasonable drag-free float in the slow current. Zip! My fly raced down stream dragging madly. On the third or fourth cast I mended the line upstream and got a longer float that drifted near an overhanging bank on my side of the stream.

Bang! A big Rainbow hit my fly. It was a number 12, grey hackle with a periwinkle blue, chenille body. I had tied that fly myself when I was a kid because I liked the blue chenille. I think I knew a girl with eyes that color.

The Rainbow jumped twice and headed north for Canada. I burned my thumb trying to slow down the whining reel. Then suddenly the tippet or the leader snapped and the fish was gone.

I sucked my legs out of the mud, losing one sneaker, and headed off for the car. Goodbye Silver Creek! What's so good about you anyway? And it was goodbye to Silver Creek for a lot of years. I put the Hemingway rod in the closet and that was that. But I was to make a return engagement many years later.

CHAPTER TWENTY-EIGHT

Ernest Hemingway throwing olives into Gary Cooper's mouth. PHOTO: AL BRACK

PAPA HEMINGWAY AND GARY COOPER

I suppose in most cases it's the father who turns his kid on to fishing. In my case it was Ernest Hemingway. My dad had a lot of passions but fishing was not one of them. When I was a kid I read Hemingway's *In Our Time* with its Nick Adams stories, and *The Sun Also Rises*, both with powerful trout fishing episodes. It wasn't long before I was tying my own flies and had received my first fly rod as a gift. It was a whippy, split bamboo pole which I still have. I'm a saver.

Hemingway was my idol. That wasn't unusual for my generation. His work spoke to many of us and it still does.

Beginning in 1939 the already famous writer went to Idaho and stayed frequently at the legendary Sun Valley resort as a non-paying, celebrity guest. He always stayed in Suite 206 of Sun Valley Lodge. That's where he wrote most of *For Whom the Bell Tolls*.

Back in 1956 when I worked as the publicist for Sun Valley I tried out the Hemingway Rod on Silver Creek. I was not successful. So I stuck the rod away in a closet and it would be many years before I fished with it again.

A few years after I worked at Sun Valley I became a press agent in Hollywood, still working for Steve Hannagan. But I missed Sun Valley and decided to go back there for a visit. I drove all the way from Southern California to the Idaho resort and checked into Sun Valley Lodge. I tried to get Suite 206 but it was occupied.

I heard that Hemingway and his wife Mary, and Gary Cooper and his wife Rocky, were staying nearby in Ketchum.

One day during my visit I hosted a cocktail party at Sun Valley Lodge. Hemingway, his movie star pal Gary Cooper, and their wives were invited and they showed up.

When the famous foursome walked into the Eddy Duchin Lounge, Mary Hemingway and Rocky Cooper saw some friends at the other end of the room and joined them. Hemingway and Cooper hung back near the entrance and I decided to take drink orders. Cooper wanted a scotch on the rocks.

"And what would you like, Papa?" I asked.

"Well, I'd like a scotch too, but if Mary sees me with one she'll kill me."

"Okay, why don't I get you a small glass of wine?"

"Get me both. You hold the scotch. I'll hold the wine."

And that's what we did. From time to time Hemingway looked over at Mary and when he thought she wasn't observing, took the scotch glass out of my hand and gave me the wine glass. Then it was scotch, wine, scotch, wine, back and forth, and the conversation picked up.

"I have a fly rod that 'Beartracks' Williams made for you. He said you didn't like it because it was too stiff, so he sold it to me for twenty five bucks," I said. I handed off the glass of scotch and took the glass of wine.

"Probably was. Catch anything with it?" Hemingway asked.

"I tried it once on Silver Creek and hooked a big Rainbow, but he got off. Too stiff I guess."

Hemingway laughed loudly and mimed the action of casting a trout fly.

As we stood there, a waiter came by with a few things to nibble—nuts and olives I recall. Hemingway and Cooper both grabbed a handful of olives and set about inventing a cocktail party game. Separated by three or four feet, they tossed olives into each other's wide open mouths. It was a sport of a highly competitive nature. Hemingway was soon ahead by several olives he had tossed into Cooper's mouth.

Then suddenly Mary and Rocky were in front of us and the game ceased.

Fortunately I was holding both the glass of scotch and the glass of wine during the olive tossing. It was time for the group to leave. Mary Hemingway directed the departure.

That was the last time I saw Hemingway.

CHAPTER TWENTY-NINE

BLUE DAMSELS AND COLD VODKA

Many years ago when I worked as publicist for Sun Valley I thought I was a hot skier and fly fisherman. On my first trip down Sun Valley's Baldy Mountain I wind-milled and dislocated my shoulder. The ski patrol took me the rest of the way down the mountain in a litter and a doctor at the Sun Valley hospital popped my shoulder back into its socket and said I was good to go. But I decided to stay off the mountain for the duration and wait for the Silver Creek fly fishing season. I did fish Silver Creek once in those days when I worked at Sun Valley. I got skunked, as fishermen say when they don't catch anything. So it was goodbye to Silver Creek for a lot of years.

A Birthday Present for my Son

Then as a birthday present for my son Jeff, who lived in Sun Valley when he was a baby, we made our return engagement. In those early days Jeff, his older brother Mike, and my wife and I lived in a log cabin in Ketchum, then a small sheep station village about two miles down the road from the Sun Valley resort.

So far I can't think of a better time in my life than those two weeks in July two years ago when Jeff and I ranged around Washington, Idaho and Montana doing some fly fishing and telling each other improbable stories of past grand exploits. It was high adventure and high drama for me. It was father and son stuff of a high order.

The weather was hot and we ate well in restaurants we found along the road. Rare steaks, pasta with red wine, and cold salads of romaine lettuce, fresh tomatoes and cucumbers, laced with olive oil and wine vinegar, all sprinkled with gorgonzola cheese and lots of ground pepper.

An Adventure in our Time

Jeff drove his small Honda SUV, and the back seat and storage area were filled with fly rods—including the one Sun Valley's famed hunting and fishing guide, Taylor "Beartracks" Williams, made for Ernest Hemingway. Beartracks had sold it to me when Hemingway didn't like its action. There was also a bag with Hemingway's *In Our Time* and *The Sun Also Rises* and dozens of magazines, mostly fishing magazines, but others on jazz, blues and rock.

On the console between the driver and passenger seats, or on the floor between my legs, were our road maps of the western states, an open shoe box filled with CDs by Stevie Ray Vaughan, Creedence Clearwater Revival and Bob Dylan—traveling music. In the glove box was a copy of Roger Tory Peterson's *A Field Guide to Western Birds*, Jeff's jack knife and a few of his good luck pieces like glassy shards of Carnelian from the Columbia River Gorge, and stones he had found on sandbars in the Yellowstone River. On the back seat were our Styrofoam cooler with cold drinks and a brown paper bag that always seemed to hold large tuna sandwiches and another bag with ripe red cherries. There was more stuff in Jeff's car but I believe that sets the stage. We were ready—for what we did not really know—but we were ready.

We drove through Washington, Idaho and Montana, fly fishing along the way. We tied bandanas around our heads like real travelers do. Of course, we had to stop in Ketchum, try to find the old log cabin on the Wood River, take a look at Sun Valley and do some fly fishing.

Jeff and I Proved You Can Go Home Again

We didn't find the old log cabin that had been on a dirt road leading to the foot of Mt. Baldy where I had dislocated my shoulder. It was long gone and the now-paved road was lined with condos. Ketchum had become a fancy town. The little sheep station village I remembered has become a sophisticated suburb of the Sun Valley resort, about two miles up the road. Ketchum is bursting at the seams with upscale restaurants, coffeehouses, wine bars, art galleries, dog grooming shops, video rental stores and, of course, real estate offices. Well, Jeff and I proved that you can go home again, but home may have changed a bit. And I had changed a bit too—a lot more birthdays, bearded now, and still with a gimpy shoulder that sometimes slipped out of its socket when I retrieved my bag at the airport.

The Blue Damsels

This time I would be fishing with the fly rod that "Beartracks" had originally made for Hemingway. And this time I booked a local fishing guide. He knew how to avoid most of the cow pies and the black mud. He stuck Jeff and me in float tubes and tied on number 12, Blue Damsel dry flies that looked like the hovering dragon flies we saw just above the surface of the stream. Floating along in the tube eliminated most of the drag that left a tell-tale V pattern on the water. Rainbow trout began rising to our flies—not fast or decisively, but tentatively and with what seemed to me, a high degree of circumspection, even amusement. Nevertheless, we each managed to catch a few careless Rainbows and work them back to the guide's net where we made a few hurried photos before we released them unharmed. At the end of the day, Silver Creek had worked for us, not like that other time so many years ago.

The Cold Vodka

Later we found an old bar on Ketchum's main drag where Hemingway used to hang out. Jeff and I ordered a couple of rare steaks and toasted Papa Hemingway and the blue damsels with cold vodka.

CHAPTER THIRTY

BUGIS STREET REVISITED

The first time I visited Singapore, many years ago, someone said, "Let's go down to Bugis Street and see what's happening." Since it was two o'clock in the morning I knew what was happening. I was drifting off, fading with jet lag. But to Bugis Street we went anyway. It was enlightening.

During the day Bugis Street, named after a tribe of out-island Malay fishermen, was just that—a street—with small shops and restaurants. But late at night, or rather early in the morning, Bugis Street made a remarkable transformation. Parked cars were removed, tables and chairs set up in the middle of the street, and the demimonde of Singapore gathered for a few educational hours over beer and noodles. For it was Bugis Street that drew Singapore's considerable transvestite community like a magnet.

To visit Bugis Street when in Singapore became a highlight, usually an innocent, but mind-boggling highlight in those days. Then in 1975 the Singapore government, as part of a sweeping modernization program, closed down Bugis Street.

But that's not the end of the tale. In 1984, bowing to what I assume was visitor demand, the Singapore government reinstated Bugis Street—or perhaps reconstituted it like frozen orange juice. The late night revels are now controlled and new visitors to Singapore somehow manage to stay awake until the wee hours and go to Bugis Street.

I did myself last visit. But it's not quite the same as it was.

CHAPTER THIRTY-ONE

THE NONYA FOOD OF THE STRAIT OF MALACCA

On a trip to George Town on the Island of Penang on the Malay Straits, I met Violet Oon, a *nonya* born in Singapore. *Nonya* is a Malay term for women. A *baba* is a man. These words refer to what are known as *Peranakan* Chinese, or Straits Settlements-born Chinese. In both Malay and Indonesian the word *Peranakan* designates "descendant" but is usually applied to Chinese immigrants who relocated from various provinces of China to the Malay Archipelago during the Chinese diaspora during the 19th century.

Peranakan Cuisine

Violet Oon was in George Town to give a cooking demonstration at my hotel. Her subject was *Peranakan* cuisine, a subtle and sophisticated mélange of traditional Chinese cuisine—Cantonese, Hokkien, Teochew, and Hainanese for example— and the cuisine of what is known as the Strait of Malacca.

Peranakan cuisine is a blend of spices and cooking techniques used by the Malays, and typical Chinese ingredients. I hung around when Violet was through with her program, sampled some of her cooking, and engaged her in conversation. Violet is a friendly lady and I convinced her I wasn't just hitting on her, and made a date to meet her back in Singapore to talk to her more about *Pernakan* cuisine.

An Aside on Singaporean Chili Crab

Violet Oon is the grande dame of Singaporean cooking—not just the *Peranakan* cooking that is very popular there—but of all Singaporean cuisine which is multi-faceted and, to my taste buds, one of the premiere cuisines in the world. I make my case by citing one Singaporean dish—Chili Crab. All outdoor "hawker" stalls in Singapore feature Chili

Crab—cracked and cleaned local crab, garlic, red chilies, spring onions, coriander, tomato ketchup, soy sauce, rice or malt vinegar. Everything is plunged into a wok and stir-fried. You eat it with your hands. When you finish a bowl of Chili Crab you will probably need to take a shower.

Once while having Chili Crab accompanied by a lot of beer at a beachside stand, I plunged into the surf—with blue jeans and t-shirt—and doused myself from head to foot. Chili Crab can have that effect on you.

Violet Oon and the Food Paper

But back to Violet Oon: She began her career in 1971 in journalism as a reporter for music and the arts on the Singapore publication *New Nation*. Soon she was given the assignment of food critic. She told me she was from a Chinese family that liked to eat (is there a Chinese family that doesn't like to eat?), and that she had been cooking seriously since the age of 15, and eating professionally since she was 23. In 1987 she launched her own publication, *The Food Paper*. It took off and she was dubbed Singapore's Food Ambassador. She has hosted her own television cooking series, is in demand as a speaker and food consultant, and has written three cookbooks.

Chinese Ingredients and Methods with Malay Spices

These days there are some top restaurants in Singapore serving *Peranakan* food. The immigrant Chinese developed a truly unique cuisine. It's ethnically Chinese, using many Chinese ingredients and cooking methods like steaming, double boiling, slow stewing, and stir frying. The *Peranakans* combine their foodstuffs and methods with the riches of the Spice Islands—cinnamon, cloves, nutmeg, mace, ginger, turmeric, galangal, lemon grass, screw pine leaf, candlenuts, pandan leaves, and coconut milk. Frequently *cinaluk* (a powerful sour and salty shrimp-based condiment) is added.

Common Nonya Dishes

Here are some examples of Peranakan cuisine as prepared by the Nonyas.

Sambal Udang—Prawns prepared Malay-Nonya style. Ingredients include Straits prawns heated over high heat in a wok with tamarind, sugar, lime juice, candlenuts, dried chilies, shrimp paste and shallots.

Babi Chin—Stewed pork in soy sauce and spices. Stir fried with garlic, shallots, green chilies, a cinnamon stick, and cloves.

Ngoh Hiang—Bean curd rolls of minced pork, prawns and crab meat. Steamed bean curd wrappers with water chestnuts, onions, soy sauce, and Chinese Five Spice powder.

Ayam Tempra—A fried chicken dish. It is prepared in a wok with onion, fresh red chilies, lime juice, and soy sauce.

Sambal Kim Chiam—A salad made with banana or lily buds. Includes prawns, cucumber, fresh red chilis, grated coconut, spice paste, shallots and a bit of sugar.

CHAPTER THIRTY-TWO

THE OLD-TIME HOLLYWOOD GLAM RESTAURANTS

Another stop on the Royal Road was Los Angeles. Actually I loved Los Angeles. I always thought LA gets a bum rap. And I say this as a San Franciscan who has delivered his share of knocks to the Southland. Many years ago I spent some time in Los Angeles, even worked there for a while as a Hollywood press agent. That gave me access to what I believe was then one of the best things about the place—its restaurants.

Now before you begin throwing punches at me for being disloyal to my city by the bay, let me add that I really believe San Francisco is one of the great restaurant towns of the world—certainly a greater restaurant town than Los Angeles. But during the time I am writing about, the early 1950s, I was an LA restaurant junkie. I ate out a lot—on the job, and as a single guy in search of nourishment. I dined around.

Where the Real LA Folks Ate

What I really want to address here is what we might term Old-Time, Hollywood Glam Restaurants—the kind where Bogie, Bacall, Errol, Groucho, and that bunch, hung out, air kissed their buddies, and dined extravagantly and expensively.

But there were many other Southland restaurants that pleased me— places where I went by myself or on dates. Here are a few I recall with pleasure: The Pantry (24-hour cops, cab drivers and other late-nighters joint in downtown LA), Musso and Frank's (Hollywood grill for the Hollywood working stiffs), Taix (French family-style, founded in 1927), Tommy's (Beverly Boulevard hamburger stand with no tables and no napkins. You sat on your car hood and devoured your chiliburger as the juices dripped down your arms), and Philippe's The Original (creator of the French dip sandwich, founded in 1908). These were the places where "real" Los Angeles folks ate—not the Hollywood glam crowd.

But the Old-Time, Hollywood Glam Restaurants, where I did my on-the-job training, were a magnificent clique of thoroughbreds: Romanoff's, Chasen's, Perino's, Scandia, and the Brown Derby.

Romanoff's and its Caviar Blinis

Prince Michael Dimitri Alexandrovich Oblensky-Romanoff, nephew to Tsar Nicholas II, reigned as Hollywood's royal-restaurateur for the movies' A-list in the 1940s and 50s. Prince Romanoff, as he called himself, was really Lithuanian-born Harry Gerguson who began his American rags-to-riches career as a Brooklyn pants presser. Hollywood went along with the joke and the stars flocked to his Beverly Hills clubby establishment. One day at lunch over caviar blinis on my press agent's expense account, Humphrey Bogart and Lauren Bacall were a few tables away—and also enjoying the caviar blinis. Romanoff's, with its phony prince, will long be remembered for a famous photograph taken there one evening. Sophia Loren, in a revealing but sedate black gown, sits staring in disbelief at her tablemate Jayne Mansfield's boobs. Unfortunately, I was not there at the time.

Chasen's and its Hobo Steak

Dave Chasen was a New York vaudeville comedian whose friend—Harold Ross, founder-editor of *The New Yorker*—encouraged him to give up comedy, move to Southern California, and open a restaurant. In fact, Ross said he and a friend would finance Chasen if he did. So in 1936 the former vaudeville comedian did just that. And the party lasted until 1995.

When it opened, Chasen's became an almost instant success. It attracted the elite of the movie world. Ronald Reagan proposed to Nancy there. Frank Sinatra, Jimmy Stewart, and Alfred Hitchcock were regulars with their own booths. Spencer Tracy, Kirk Douglas, and Lana Turner hung out there. When Liz Taylor was filming *Cleopatra* with her lover, Richard Burton, she had Chasen's chili jetted to her in Rome. I never had Chasen's chili flown to me but I was lucky enough to dine at his restaurant once in a while and I favored the Hobo Steak—a salt encrusted New York strip finished at your table in brown butter. I was not exactly a hobo but I loved it.

Perino's, where Hitchcock, Sinatra and other Hollywood royalty dined. PHOTO: FRED LYON

At Chasen's the idea was to sit in the rectangular room right off the entryway. It featured green leather booths and framed movie star photos. The back room, also with framed photos (B list, I suppose), with red leather booths, was also always occupied. Nevertheless, it was referred to as "Fresno" by general manager and principal door stopper, Ronnie Clint, whom it was important to know.

The Elegant Pink and Peach Perino's

Perino's was perhaps the most elegant of the Hollywood Glam joints with its peach and pink color scheme. It was the place where one saw Hitchcock, Sinatra, Kirk Douglas, Gregory Peck, and other silver screen superstars. Entering Perino's was a theatrical event. After passing muster, you were ushered like an eastern potentate (there is no other way to describe your entrance) into a large oval room. In its center were four tufted, peach and pink taffeta booths with oval tables set with pink linen. Around the perimeter were more of the same.

The menu at Perino's was vaguely Italian—veal parmigiana, gnocchi Piedmontese—that kind of thing. But it was not too Italian, and it included elaborate French dishes like *canard a l'orange*, flamed at your table.

Early in my Hollywood days (make that daze) I drove a Fiat Topolino, the tiniest and most plebian of foreign autos. But the Perino's parking lot attendants didn't seem to mind, as long as I tipped big. Later, when good fortune smiled on me for a while, I graduated to a Mark 7 Jaguar; they liked me even better and left my car right in front of the doorway. Ah those were the days (again, let's make that daze).

Scandia and its Gravlax with Aquavit

Scandia, another Hollywood hangout, was a glass enclosed aerie perched on Sunset Boulevard in West Hollywood. It was founded in 1946 by a Dane from Copenhagen named Ken Hansen who served fine Scandinavian cuisine to Hollywood's rich and famous. Upon entering, you were faced with a handsome bar that John Wayne liked. Wayne—his real name was Marion Morrison—could be seen there frequently with a group of his movie buddies. When I saw him there he didn't seem as tall as I thought he looked on the screen.

My favorite dish at Scandia was gravlax and mustard sauce with small wedges of black bread. It was served with a shot of aquavit. Scandia made its own gravlax and I was able to coax the recipe out of Hansen. Filets of wild salmon are sandwiched with fresh dill, sugar, salt and pepper. Aquavit is poured over it and it is refrigerated and "cured" for at least three days. I still prepare it and sip a little aquavit while doing so in remembrance of days gone by. Scandia finally closed in 1989.

The Brown Derby and the Cobb Salad

The Brown Derby, on Vine Street in Hollywood, was populated by movie greats. It is said that Clark Gable proposed to Carole Lombard there. My first day on the job with the Steve Hannagan organization—a Hollywood publicity firm—my boss took me to lunch at the Brown Derby. Groucho Marx sat alone in the next booth. The captain brought a black telephone with a long cord over to Groucho's table, plugged it into a wall socket and Groucho did some business I couldn't pick up as I tried to eavesdrop.

I had the Cobb Salad. That's what you were supposed to have at the Brown Derby. The Cobb Salad may have been the first chopped salad.

It was named for Robert Cobb, Brown Derby proprietor. It was a large, plated salad with a variety of finely chopped this-and-that—iceberg and Romaine lettuce, watercress, endive, tomato, bacon, chicken or turkey breast, hard-boiled egg, avocado, chives and Roquefort cheese. The dressing was a red wine vinaigrette.

These places were expensive. You didn't dine there on your bubblegum money. My viewpoint is they were expensive but worth it. The food was memorable, and for sheer theater (in this case moving picture theatrics) it was incomparable. But, when on my own dime, you could usually find me at Musso and Frank's on Hollywood Boulevard.

CHAPTER THIRTY-THREE

MEDITERRANEAN MISCELLANY

Over the years I have been fortunate to spent a considerable time sailing on *Mare Nostrum* (our sea), as the Romans called the Mediterranean. Laying at the juncture of three continents—Europe, Africa and Asia—the Mediterranean is the highway upon which western civilization was founded. I have experienced the Mediterranean by sea and along the lands that edge it. Azure blue seascapes, golden beaches, rocky cliffs, volcanic stepping-stone islands, and great and dramatic cities.

The Mediterranean is a legendary sea, but by comparison with others, it's a small one. Lawrence Durrell in his superb novel *Balthazar*, said, "The Mediterranean is an absurdly small sea; the length and greatness of its history makes us dream it larger than it is."

And, it is enjoyable to read about *Mare Nostrum* in books like Durrell's *Balthazar a*nd to dream of being there. Long ago to help me conjure, or dream, about the Mediterranean I kept a journal I called "Mediterranean Miscellany." What follows are a few of my entries.

The Middle of the Earth
The word "Mediterranean" means middle of the earth. And so it was to the ancients who crisscrossed her waters in battle and in trade.

Byron and Homer Can't Seem to Get the Color Right
Perhaps a good way to get in the mood for a Mediterranean sojourn is to read Lord Byron, the romantic poet who traced an odyssey through the countries bordering the Mediterranean in his extended poem *Childe Harold's Pilgrimage*, and that wandering Homer's *Odyssey*. Byron conceived a beautiful line, "*Roll on thou deep and dark blue ocean—roll.* And Homer referred to the Mediterranean in the *Odyssey* as the "*wine dark sea.*" Apparently the color is in the eye of the beholder.

Here Were Probably the First Ships to Venture Forth

The Mediterranean Sea nurtured many nations of mariners. The first to build seagoing vessels were the Egyptians. In fact the earliest known record of ships comes from Egypt. The Egyptians made coastal voyages along the African shores of the sea. A tomb inscription describes "the loading of the ships very heavily with marvels of the country of Punt (probably Somaliland); all goodly fragrant woods of God's Land, heaps of myrrh-resin, with fresh myrrh trees (myrrh was in great demand as a perfume and as one of the ingredients used by the Egyptian royal embalmers), with ebony and pure ivory, with green gold of emu, with cinnamon wood, khesyt wood, with ihmut-incense, sonter-incense, eye cosmetic, with apes, monkeys, dogs, and with skins of the southern panther, with natives and their children...."

Red Roofs against a Blue Sea

Through the ages artists have flocked to the shores of the Mediterranean. Joseph M.A. Turner, the Englishman, anticipated the Impressionists and painted seascapes of an heroic, nevertheless, evanescent quality. Cezanne wrote to Pizarro who was in Paris: "It is like a playing card, red roofs against the blue sea. The sun was so terrific that it seems to me as if the objects were silhouetted not only in black and white, but in blue, red, brown and violet." Monet, Renoir, Picasso, Dali, Matisse, Chagall, and Van Gogh—the Mediterranean light inspired them all.

Venice is the Chocolate Liqueur of Cities

Great cities and city states such as Venice grew to become powerful because of their access to the Mediterranean, prompting great merchant families and trading houses. Venice was referred to by John Addington Symonds as "The Shakespeare of Cities—unchallenged, incomparable, and beyond envy." Henry Wadsworth Longfellow referred to Venice as the "White Swan of Cities." Later Truman Capote said "Venice is like eating an entire box of chocolate liqueurs at one go."

Of Bouillabaisse there is Some Dispute

There's a story that bouillabaisse was first prepared by the goddess

Venus to put her spouse Vulcan to sleep so she could continue a rendezvous with Mars. Arguments abound about bouillabaisse. Just what should it include? Lobster? No, say purists. Tomatoes? Perhaps. A pinch of saffron? Probably yes. Bouillabaisse is ever-present along the European shores of the Mediterranean. When seen on menus—especially in Marseilles—it should be ordered immediately.

Churchill and Brigitte Bardot

Brigitte Bardot practically invented St. Tropez that slithers along the shore of the Mediterranean. Before she visited, it was a sleepy village. She once met Sir Winston Churchill there and told him she was a painter. The great statesman also loved to paint the Mediterranean. She told Churchill that unlike him, she hadn't won any wars. He replied, "That's no great loss."

The Mediterranean Bookbag:

Besides Lawrence Durrell's *Balthazar* from his linked novels of *The Alexandria Quartet*—*Justine, Balthazar, Mountolive,* and *Clea*—here are a few books I pack in my Mediterranean bookbag:

Death in Venice by Thomas Mann (dark and sinister account of a fatal attraction), *The Pillars of Hercules* by Paul Theroux (he circled most of the Mediterranean, on foot, by train, local ferry, and cruise ship), *A Year in Provence* by Peter Mayle (required reading for visitors to Provence), *The Civilization of the Renaissance in Italy* by Jacob Burckhardt (I've never been able to find anyone who has read this cover-to-cover, but browsing is rewarding. Morality, religion, society, festivals, artists, and the demimonde), *Suetonius's Lives of the Twelve Caesars* by, of course, Suetonius (this is the classic book on the Roman nobility that dishes out all the dirt.

Suetonius was the private secretary to Emperor Hadrian. He was in a good spot to pick up facts and rumors from the servants and savants. If you want a behind-the-scenes look at Julius's liveliest fancy, Cleopatra, dip into Suetonius. Anything you've always wanted to know about Tiberius, Claudius, or Nero, read Suetonius. *Italy, the Places Between* by Kate Simon (she was a travel writer who had no peer. She died too

Henry Miller's book, *The Colossus of Maroussi* shimmers with life. PHOTO: FRED LYON

early. This is the quintessential Italy), *Two Towns in Provence* by M.F.K. Fisher (Fisher was the ultimate prose stylist whether writing about food or about the people who create it. When you read her you automatically become hungry), *The Colossus of Maroussi* by Henry Miller (no, don't expect Miller's epic, sexual "tropic" wanderings. Miller wrote this book about Greece and its people. It shimmers with life).

CHAPTER THIRTY-FOUR

AT MY TABLE

The Palm

Many years ago when I worked in New York City for *Collier's Magazine* I hung out at the Palm on Second Avenue. I met one of the owners, Wally Ganzi, and we hit it off. If you were a regular at the Palm, you called it Ganzi's—much like in San Francisco, if you were a regular at the old Washington Square Bar & Grill, you called it the Square. So I had juice at this seminal steak and lobster house that took no reservations. When I was going to Ganzi's for those three and four pound lobsters, Wally Ganzi, descendant of the original owner, John Ganzi, operated only one restaurant. Later he and his partner, a descendant of a co-founder, opened Palm Too on Second Avenue right across the street from the original. Today, the heirs have a bunch of restaurants.

In the 1920s John Ganzi and Pio Bozzi, recent immigrants from Parma, Italy, wanted to open a restaurant so they applied for a business license. They wanted to call their restaurant Parma, but the city official couldn't understand their fractured English and he wrote: "Palm" on the license. So it's Palm today and it's my favorite New York joint.

Luk Yu Tea House

I used to go to Hong Kong two or three times a year. There are many fine restaurants in Hong Kong but my favorite place was the Luk Yu Tea House, which opened in 1933. It's located in the Central District of Hong Kong Island and is a throwback to colonial times—dark woodwork, stained glass murals, and brass spittoons, and ceiling fans. Lots of atmosphere! The old place is known for its dim sum, which is first rate. If dim sum is not your style there are some very good noodle dishes and my favorite, salt and pepper chicken wings. When I was going there the checker still toted up your bill on an abacus.

Musso and Frank's Grill

Musso and Frank's Grill was, and still is, an old-time Hollywood hangout. When I was a Hollywood press agent I ate there with my boss, Steve Hannagan, and his red-haired, movie star girlfriend, Ann Sheridan. Opened in 1919 by Joseph Musso and Frank Toulet, it was located right across Hollywood Boulevard from the Screen Writers Guild and attracted a lot of movie writers including F. Scott Fitzgerald, William Faulkner, and Raymond Chandler. That was before my time, but I did meet the big band leader Stan Kenton there.

When I worked as a press agent my office was in a Snow White and the Seven Dwarfs courtyard of cottages on Sunset Boulevard. Musso and Frank's was just a few blocks away. A lot of press agents ate there because it was always full of Hollywood insiders, and served plain but excellent food—good steaks and chops—and poured serviceable martinis. I still go there these days when, for some obscure reason, I find myself in Southern California. It looks the same as it did when I was a press agent—lots of mahogany and worn, red leather booths.

Brasserie Lipp

Whenever I'm in Paris—not too often unfortunately—I skip the big-time restaurants, and hurry over to the Boulevard Saint-Germaine and drop into Brasserie Lipp for a beer, a sausage with remoulade sauce, and some potato salad. That's my standard meal at this famed Alsatian landmark founded in 1880. And why is that my standard meal at Brasserie Lipp? In Ernest Hemingway's *A Moveable Feast*, his recollections of Paris when he was there in the twenties when he had little money and frequently went hungry, he wrote about Brasserie Lipp: "The beer was very cold and wonderful to drink. The *pommes a l'huile* were firm and marinated in the olive oil. Delicious…. When the *pommes a l'hiuile* were gone I ordered another serving and a *cervelas*. This was a sausage like a heavy, wide frankfurter split in two and covered with a special mustard sauce."

Sam's Grill

A bit of history will help to fix Sam's Grill and Seafood Restaurant in San Francisco restaurant lore. Tadich Grill dates its founding to 1849, the Old Clam House to 1861, Sam's Grill (my favorite old-timer) to 1867, Fior D' Italia to 1886, and Schroeder's to 1893. Sam's opened as an oyster saloon. Later it was operated by Sam Zenovich and was called the Reception Café, but most customers called it Sam's. It changed hands in 1937 and became Sam's Grill and Seafood Restaurant. It moved to its present Bush Street location in 1946. A few years ago Sam's almost went down the drain. A small group of regulars took it over and saved it. What was saved?—those private, curtained booths for those who require discretion, and the freshest seafood to be found. I go there for the fried clams, the charcoal broiled Petrale, the hash browns, and the creamed spinach.

Les Crayeres

The fanciest restaurant I ever dined in was Les Crayeres. It's located in a magnificent mansion in France's Champagne region about an hour from Paris. It was built in 1904 for the prominent Pommery Champagne family. My wife, our daughter, and I were going to be passing through Reims on our way to visit relatives in Alsace. We decided to stop over at Les Crayeres as a luxury indulgence and we booked a suite at what was then called Boyer Les Crayeres. Gerard Boyer, then being the chef at the three Michelin-starred restaurant. We presented ourselves mid-afternoon and were given a corner suite overlooking the estate's 17-acre, walled park. We toured the grounds, poked around in the mansion and relaxed in our suite until it was time to go to dinner.

Our meal was simple but elegant; mine was a wild sea bass served with crayfish and tender white asparagus. Wife and daughter raved about their roast duckling. Specifics of our meals are lost in time. But I do recall an incident that occurred during our meal. Do you like dog stories? Well, here's one for you.

At a nearby table there was an extremely fashionable couple enjoying a bottle—perhaps two—of Pommery Metropole, which, at the time, seemed to be the Champagne of choice at Boyer Les Crayeres. Suddenly a tuxedoed waiter appeared at their table. He held aloft a small tray topped by a silver bell. He removed the bell at held its contents

John Lewis, pianist and director for the Modern Jazz Quartet.
PHOTO: FROM THE COLLECTION OF ERNEST BEYL

so madame could view it. Then with her approval, he set it on the fine Persian rug beneath their table for the small, Bichon Frise sitting there at ease. We all dined together.

Josy-Jo

In the foothills above the Cote d'Azur, a few miles from Nice, there is a medieval village called Cagnes sur Mer—a storybook place with old stone buildings with iron-barred windows and red-tiled roofs, standing on cobbled lanes. Impressionist master painter, Pierre-Auguste Renoir occupied one in his later years, and Modigliani lived for a while in the old stone building now occupied by the nearby restaurant Josy-Jo, which opened in 1970.

John Lewis, pianist and musical director for the Modern Jazz Quartet, loved this Provencal region and bought an old stone house in Cagnes sur Mer where he liked to vacation. I was fortunate to count John Lewis as a friend, and many years ago visited him when he was in residence in the village.

One fine evening he took me out to dinner right down the cobbled street from his house. And I remember the meal I had at Josy-Jo with John. We began with grilled red peppers topped with a fragrant local olive oil. This we accompanied with pink Bandol rose. There followed a roast leg of baby lamb. The whole roast was brought to our table and was sliced and plated tableside. It was pink and garlicky, with au jus moistening the meat. On the same plate was a mound of delicious white beans. I divined they were cooked with a leftover roast leg of lamb bone from a previous day. A few cloves had been added to the au jus. With this we sipped a modest red wine I can't remember too well. It was a glorious meal with a wonderful friend. After we dined John walked me back to his house, sat down at a grand piano and played a little Chopin for me—stately at first, but then with the bebop cadence John Lewis was famous for.

CHAPTER THIRTY-FIVE

JEFF ENCOUNTERS HONG KONG

My son Jeff was divorced in 1985 and was rattling around in apathy. He needed cheering up, and I thought I knew what would do the job. I gave him a call and said "I have to go to Hong Kong in a few weeks. Why don't you go with me?" At first he was doubtful, but soon he warmed up to the idea. But a problem arose. We're talking here about a young man who had no passport. Jeff's only ventures outside of the U.S. had been to Tijuana to the bullfights, and to Vancouver, B.C. to visit friends. We sorted out the passport situation, and one day flew to Hong Kong. During the flight I told Jeff, "This trip will change your life."

When our flight arrived, late at night, a chauffeur-driven, British racing green Rolls Royce from the Peninsula Hotel whisked us into the city and we checked in.

Jeff was exhausted and after he looked out the window to Hong Kong Harbor and the island of Victoria across the water, he fell into bed. Before he crashed I just had time to say "Tomorrow morning I have to go over to the Government Information Services offices in Central. Do you want to go with me or shall I let you sleep in?" No sleeping in for this kid. He was set for adventure.

Chan Sau-king

The following morning we took the Star Ferry across Hong Kong Harbor. Chinese junks moved along in a stately manner, lighters bumped up against anchored freighters to unload cargo, sampans scooted along this way and that. In a few minutes we disembarked and made our way to the G.I.S. offices on Lockhart Road. At that period of my life I was doing some public relations work for the colonial Hong Kong Government and I had an appointment to talk to some contacts there. I announced myself and soon we were joined in the lobby by a young Chinese woman, Chan Sau-king.

She was an information officer for G.I.S. and I was there to see her boss. The three of us stood talking for a few minutes and then someone came to get me. Before I left I asked Sau-king if she could look after Jeff while I was gone. Of course, she would, and I left.

Forty or so minutes later my meeting was finished and I went back to the lobby. There they were chatting easily. We said goodbye to Sau-king and left.

I then took Jeff over to the Hong Kong Foreign Correspondent's Club on Lower Albert Road. After checking in we sat at the big oval bar and drank beer.

It was then that Jeff turned to me and said, "Dad, if I wanted to write to that girl, how would I do that?"

"What girl?" I replied.

He was jet lagged and didn't think that was funny. I gave him the information.

Our Spirits Rose

We stayed in Hong Kong at the "Pen" for a week. I showed him everything I liked about the incredible city—Aberdeen where the boat people lived, the floating restaurants, Au Boon Haw's Tiger Balm Gardens, Mongkok, the world's most crowded urban district, antique shops on Hollywood Road, restaurants and bars.   I even took him up to Lo Wu by train where we peeked across the border into China.

Jeff had a great time. He spirits were raised. My spirits were already on steroids and I had a great time too.

Jeff Had a Friend in Town

We flew back to San Francisco—back to the real world. Jeff lived in Berkeley, had a job and I didn't see him often. We talked on the telephone occasionally, and that was that.

Then one day—perhaps a year after the Hong Kong trip—Jeff called. Remember this was more than 30 years ago, but I remember the conversation verbatim.

Jeff and Chan Sau-king. PHOTO: COURTESY JEFF BEYL

"Hi Dad, I haven't seen you in a while," Jeff said.

"Yeah, what are you doing with yourself?" I said.

"Not much," he said.

"Why don't you come over one of these days? It's been a long time," I said.

"Okay," he said.

"Why don't you come over this weekend? Come early so we can talk, then we'll have dinner," I said.

"Okay, but I have a friend in town," he said.

To show you what kind of guy I was, I said "Bring him over," and we made the date.

That Sunday, at the appointed time, the doorbell rang. I opened the door. There standing on the porch was Jeff—six feet, five inches in his stocking feet. Standing beside him was Chan Sau-king—perhaps five feet plus.

I didn't have a clue. In all those months he hadn't said a word.

Fade Out, Fade In

Another year went by. One day Jeff called me.

"Dad," he said, getting directly to the point. "What would you say if I told you I wanted to marry Sau-king?"

"I would say it would be a great idea," I said.

"Okay then, Jeff said.

I was Best Man at their wedding.

CHAPTER THIRTY-SIX

SHOPPING IS THERAPY
RAISED TO THE TENTH POWER

I'm not a world-class shopper, but once in a while I get lucky. Let me give you a few examples:

Several years ago in Hong Kong I interviewed Lord Kadoorie for a magazine piece I had in mind. The piece was going to be on Hong Kong's famed Peninsula Hotel which the Kadoorie family owned. So Lawrence Kadoorie, industrialist, intellectual, philanthropist, and British Lord, invited me around to his office for a chat. I sat opposite the courtly old man at a large antique Chinese table he used as a desk. Between us, balanced carelessly on a stack of paper work, was a magnificent, obviously ancient, pottery horsehead.

"Han Dynasty," said Lord Kadoorie noticing my attention. "About 200 B.C. to 200 A.D. They were funeral objects entombed with wealthy Chinese nobles."

"Got to get me one of those," I said flippantly.

"Oh, you can find them here—perhaps up on Hollywood Road," he said, and we went ahead with the interview.

A few days later I walked into a dusty shop on Hollywood Road and told the proprietor that Lord Kadoorie had sent me to look at some Han Dynasty horseheads. Obviously pleased, and thinking Lord Kadoorie had sent me, the shopkeeper brought out several examples and lined them up on a velvet cloth for me to study. An hour later I walked out of the shop with my very own Han Dynasty horsehead packed for travel, along with an official certificate of authenticity. Although my credit card was limp and reeling from the blow, I'm convinced the shopkeeper gave me a good price because I invoked the name of the man so well respected in Hong Kong. Today I think of the horsehead—sitting on my desk as I write this—as one of the great shopping scores of my life. Such are the joys of travel.

Browsing the World's Bazaars

For me, and perhaps most travelers, shopping ranks only a percentage point or so behind sampling exotic foreign cuisine. Visiting temples, palaces, and cathedrals is probably number three. But successful shopping while traveling usually takes a lot of research and energy. You don't always get lucky. When you browse the world's bazaars, flea markets, high rise emporiums, and exclusive shops when traveling, you'll always find wonderful local treasures along with the obligatory straw hats, t-shirts and other souvenir stuff. In Hong Kong it may be the Han horseheads, blue-and-white porcelain ginger jars, or high fashion items. But let's bounce around the globe a bit with a few shopping ideas that might strike your fancy.

Paper, Glass and Masks in Venice

Consider Venice. Here for the compulsive shopper, the one who considers shopping while traveling to be therapy raised to the tenth power, the choices are many and varied. But I confidently narrow the choices down to paper, glass and masks. Along the Venice canals are small shops selling truly exquisite handmade paper—stationery, gift wrappings, leather-bound diaries, address books and the like. And Venetian glass vases, bottles, and even chandeliers are fine prizes to take home. But perhaps the most striking of Venice's take home treasures are the finely made *papier-mache* carnival masks the locals wear during the three-day, Venice *Carnevale*.

Bangkok for Thai Silk

To continue this peripatetic shopping spree, in Bangkok you may want to skip the phony Rolex watches and stop by Jim Thompson's Thai Silk store. (As you will read elsewhere on these pages Jim Thompson was the American who revitalized the art of silk weaving in Thailand and later went missing in Malaysia's Cameron Highlands.) Thai silk with its iridescent shimmer, makes incredibly beautiful decorative pillows, table cloths, napkins and all manner of fancy garments. It became wildly popular in the United States when it was used for the costumes in the original version of the musical *The King and I*. Bangkok is also a fine spot to shop for such items as antique *Bencharong* bowls and plates. The five-colored porcelain was originally made in China but shipped to old Siam (now known as Thailand) for purchase and use by the color-loving Siamese.

Istanbul for Evil Eye Beads

What to buy in the Grand Bazaar of Istanbul might be a question with which you have been wrestling? Evil Eye beads could be one choice that would be perfect as a conversational opener back home. These strings of blue glass beads guard one against the notorious Evil Eye. Wherever travelers wander in this part of the world talismans such as Evil Eye beads can be found. Buy some and find out whether they work better than a rabbit's foot, or a four-leaf clover on your key chain.

Elsewhere: Opals, Paintings, Sandalwood Figurines, Marmalade, Jewelry, Art Prints, and Cashmere

Australia? Opals are a good choice. Most come from Australia's Coober Pedy mines. Aboriginal bark paintings are good buys too.

The Island of Bali? What comes to mind are sandalwood figurines of traditional Balinese dancers, and Brueghel-like, people-swarming paintings from the artists' colony at Ubud.

London? Easy! Thick cut marmalade from Fortnum and Mason, and cashmere sweaters from the Burlington Arcade are at the top of my list.

The Greek Islands? Bold handmade jewelry set with semi-precious stones.

Paris? Fine art prints from the Louvre. Handmade shoes from the Left Bank. Old French language books from the outdoor stalls along the Seine.

But remember, these are just one traveler's choices. Readers will want to do their own research. But that's the point, isn't it?

THE BROTH OF CHINESE HISTORY

I'm a sucker for chicken soup. I love it even when I'm not in bed with a bad cold and require large doses of "Jewish Penicillin" to set me right. So wherever I travel I check out the chicken soup. So far, the best I've had is in China.

Why is that? I asked my friend Eileen Yin-fei Lo, a Chinese cookbook author who knows about these things.

Eileen explained to me that throughout Chinese history, the royalty insisted on the best chicken soup that could be conceived. In the Emperor's household an army of cooks prepared delicacies for the royal family. Included was the chicken broth of the gods. It was called Number One Supreme Chicken Soup.

Here is how Eileen Yin-fei Lo described it for me:

A Soup for Confucius, Genghis Khan, The Dowager Empress, Sun Yatsen, Mao Zedong, and Deng Xiaoping

"I have it on the best authority that all Chinese historical personages had a common love of soup. Yet how are we to put together this broth of history? It should, of course, be satisfying both to the gentle aesthetics of Confucius, and the brawny appetite of Genghis Khan. Its flavor must be such that the Dowager Empress would be pleased, and so would her less gentle successors Sun Yatsen and Mao Zedong. And I take Deng Xiaoping at his word: 'It doesn't matter whether the cat is black or white, as long as it catches mice.' The soup therefore, must be one that fits into the whole panoply of Chinese history. What better than a chicken soup, a universal, the best chicken soup, the number one chicken soup, the Number One Supreme Chicken Soup?"

Number One Supreme Chicken Soup

Recipes from the Chinese Imperial Dynasties are scant, and that of the Number One Supreme Chicken Soup is not available to chicken soup scholars. So we asked Eileen Yin-fei Lo to recreate how it may have been prepared. Here is her recipe:

Ingredients

7 pounds chicken bones and skins
10 cups water
Additional 3 quarts very cold water
1 piece of fresh ginger, 1 inch thick, lightly smashed
2 garlic cloves peeled
4 scallions
2 medium sized onions, peeled and quartered
Salt to taste

Method

Bring 10 cups of water to a boil in a large pot.

–Add chicken bones and skin and allow to boil for one minute . Turn off the heat and pour off the water. Run cold water over the skin and bones to clean them.

–Place skin and bones in a large stockpot. Add 3 quarts of cold water, ginger, garlic, scallions, onions, and salt. Cover and bring to a boil. Partially uncover stockpot, and allow to simmer for 3 ½ to 4 hours.

–Strain contents and reserve the stock. Discard solid ingredients.

–Place stock in a large pot with 3 cups of water and add,

–3/4 pound of lean pork cut into cubes.

–Return soup to a boil, lower heat, cover pot, and simmer for five minutes.

–Add ½ pound fresh mushrooms, and allow broth to come to a boil again.

–Add 2 medium carrots sliced thin. Return to boil.

–Add ¼ pound snow peas. Return to boil.

–Add four cakes of fresh bean curd cut into ½ inch cubes. Return to boil.

–Turn off heat and add 2 tablespoons of soy sauce, and 2 tablespoons of sesame oil.

–Stir well and serve.

CHAPTER THIRTY-EIGHT

The Cathedral of Santiago de Compostela. PHOTO: FRED LYON

SANTIAGO DE COMPOSTELA

I wish I could write here that I journeyed to the Spanish city, Santiago de Compostela, by walking hundreds of miles on a pilgrimage—maybe even moving painfully forward on my knees as some worshippers have done since the Middle Ages. But I can't. I took a bus from La Coruna on the Galician Atlantic coast of Spain—a city with a buzzing nightlife I enjoyed.

Santiago de Compostela began as a Roman cemetery. Throughout the ages many conquerors occupied the site—the Visigoths, the Vikings, the Portuguese, the French, and finally the Spanish.

The Way of St. James

The origins of Santiago de Compostela are found in its cathedral where St. James the apostle is believed buried. The Catholic pilgrimage to this sacred shrine originated in the 9th Century and is known as The Way of St. James. At some time between 818 AD and 842 AD, Bishop Theodomir of Iria Flavia, in what is now northwest Spain, found what he believed to be the bones of Saint James. Legend says that after preaching in Galicia, Saint James returned to the Holy Land where he was captured and beheaded. His followers stole his body from the authorities, and after many trials, took it to the site of what is now Santiago de Compostela. And that's how the pilgrimages began. Today, approximately 100,000 pilgrims travel each year to the city from all over Europe and elsewhere.

Santiago de Compostela

The city itself is of considerable interest, and would be even if there were no cathedral. There are elegant buildings, including a baroque abbey and city hall, and the 16th Century University of Santiago de Compostela.

The Cathedral of Santiago de Compostela

When I went there, I think it was in 1970 or thereabouts, I was not really on a pilgrimage. I was curious to see the sights and sounds—perhaps I was tiring of La Coruna. I stayed in a *parador* and dined in local restaurants. During the day I explored the city on foot. The cathedral is huge and elaborate. What began as an ancient shrine became a Romanesque church in 829 AD. Construction of the present cathedral—Gothic with baroque touches—began in 1075. It was consecrated in 1211.

While Pilgrimages did—and still can—begin anywhere, there are a few principal routes. One is a journey from Le Puy in southern France. Others are from Saint-Jean-Pied-de-Port in the Pyrenees foothills on the French side, or from the town of Roncesvalles on the Spanish side,

Although I hadn't made a pilgrimage, I was eager to see the cathedral. That's really what it's all about in Santiago de Compostela. It turned out to be my lucky day since it was a special "feast" day that I have now forgotten. I joined a flock of worshippers and just plain tourists like myself.

The famous *Botafumeiro* (incense dispenser) of Santiago de Compostela.
PHOTO: FRED LYON

I entered and walked up purposively to the third row of pews and sat down next to the aisle. I like aisle seats in churches, theaters, and symphony halls—easy to escape, if escape is your thing. In the Cathedral of Santiago de Compostela I didn't want to escape. But later I wondered about my choice of an aisle position. Here's why.

Dispensing the Incense

The Catholic mass I viewed turned out to be more than I had planned on. All of the pomp and circumstance was there, but also something I didn't count on—a whiff of danger. As many readers will know there is an interval during the ritual of the mass when a priest walks among the parishioners waving a thurible—an elaborate dispenser—that emits clouds of smoky incense amidst the worshippers. In the liturgy of the mass, the incense represents an important element—a prayer to the Almighty. In the 11th Century the Cathedral of Santiago de Compostela added a dramatic and novel twist on the idea of dispensing incense.

The Botafumeiro of Santiago de Compostela

The famous thurible of the cathedral is called Botafumeiro (smoke expeller). This thurible is huge—one of the largest in the world. It weighs more than 175 pounds and is more than five feet in height and is used on important occasions according to church calendar. The Botafumeiro is attached by a thick rope that is wound around a large pulley hanging just below the cathedral's ceiling. Eight men, red-robed *tiraboleiros* (incense carriers) set the Botafumeiro in motion by hoisting it to the ceiling and then pulling and giving way on the rope so it begins swinging in an arc. As they continue, the huge censer swings in greater arcs until it almost reaches the ceiling.

At its maximum it swings from the transept behind the alter, down a few feet from the floor (adjacent to where I was sitting on the aisle), and then continues its dramatic arc upwards to the ceiling, somewhere to the rear of the church. During its tremendous journey it emits heavy clouds of incense. This is alarmingly dramatic and got my heart pounding.

Is it dangerous to swing this huge thurible? Well, there have been accidents over the years. In 1499 the Botofumeiro broke loose and flew out of a cathedral window, and there have been a few other mishaps, but nothing fatal. Along the way, if it had beaned a pilgrim he or she would have been assured of passage through those Pearly Gates right then and there.

CHAPTER THIRTY-NINE

The author in a bar at the Oceano Hotel in Puerto Vallarta.
PHOTO: FROM THE COLLECTION OF ERNEST BEYL

LIZ AND DICK AT GRINGO GULCH

Back in the 1950s and -60s I spent a few weeks each year in Puerto Vallarta. The Pacific coastal town was a laid-back oasis then. It was a fine place to go when you wanted your motor to idle. A friend from San Francisco—the industrial designer Walter Landor—had a villa in Puerto Vallarta, and when he wasn't using it (which seemed to be most of the time) it was mine for the asking. And I asked a lot.

The Walter Landor villa—and it was truly a villa—was a two-story, multi-bedroom place spread around an open-to-the-sky, interior courtyard. It was in this courtyard that I dined lavishly on fresh fish, and held court with Mexican and San Francisco friends.

The villa was located in what was called Gringo Gulch. I don't know what Gringo Gulch is like now, or if it even still exists, but in those days it was a barren gulch running almost from the center of town up into the adjoining hills. A small, lively stream ran through Gringo Gulch, and in the mornings Mexican women washed their household clothing in the stream's pools, then wringing them out and beating them against the rocks.

A Voluptuous Lifestyle

Those were good days for me in PV—as we called Puerto Vallarta. The villa came equipped with a cook, a gardener, and what I suppose we could call a houseboy. Cook, gardener, and houseboy today seem societally out of reach or incorrect to most of us. The very words are now so stigmatized that I almost hesitate to use them here. But my lifestyle in Gringo Gulch was grand. I ate a lot of ceviche, and drank a lot of tequila with sangrita chasers, and a lot of margaritas. It was a voluptuous lifestyle.

Liz and Dick in Residence

The lovers Elizabeth Taylor and Richard Burton also had a villa in Gringo Gulch. It was the next villa up from Landor's along a winding, cobblestoned lane. I was told about the presence of Liz and Dick when I first began going to Puerto Vallarta. But whenever I was there they didn't seem to be in residence.

Liz and Dick a few Tables Away

When I was in Puerto Vallarta I descended from my Gringo Gulch villa from time to time, walking down the winding trail to make or receive long distance telephone calls. It was necessary at that time to go to a central telephone exchange in town to do this. And sometimes I would leave my lavish premises to visit friends in a town bar or restaurant. One place I liked to go to was the Oceano Hotel on the *malecon*, Puerto Vallarta's waterfront promenade. And one day while I was sitting in the breezy barroom there, I looked up from my beer and there they were—Liz and Dick—just a few tables away.

John Huston's The Night of the Iguana

Later, when I told this story—and I told it a lot—I explained that Richard Burton, the classic British actor, was in Mexico to star in a role in the John Huston movie *The Night of the Iguana*. Burton's co-star was Ava Gardner, and Elizabeth Taylor was jealous and hung around the set pouting and keeping an eagle eye out for trouble. And trouble was Ava Gardner's middle name.

Intrigue at Mismaloya

Huston was shooting the Tennessee Williams play a few miles south of Puerto Vallarta at Mismaloya, a tiny promontory on a secluded beach. Nothing was there at the time—no hotel, no water supply, and therefore, no tourists—perfect for Huston to film his movie. And perfect, I suppose, for Hollywood Intrigue. Taylor was in the midst of a torrid affair with Burton who was soon to be her fifth husband.

Knocking Back Tequila Shots at the Oceano

All of this was in my mind as I viewed Liz and Dick not far from me in the Oceano. There they were knocking back tequila shots with beer chasers. It was late afternoon and there was a glorious sunset out over the bay. And I was emboldened by the fiery view, and by the beer. I stood up shakily, walked over to their table, and introduced myself. After all, we were neighbors, weren't we? I must have been a charming son-of-a-bitch in those days because they asked me to join them. Soon we were on a first name basis—Liz, Dick, and Ernie. But they more properly called me Ernesto. We sat and drank until almost dark.

Then Burton said to me, "Where are you staying? "

"Gringo Gulch," I replied. "Just below you."

"Are you from that place below us that's making all the noise?" he asked.

I was.

"Let's go then," Burton said. And we lurched to our feet, walked out, and headed for home. There was no use getting a taxi. They couldn't drive up Gringo Gulch.

Richard Burton and Elizabeth Taylor in *Cleopatra*.
PHOTO: THE COURIER-GAZETTE / WIKIMEDIA COMMONS

Up Gringo Gulch with My New Friends

Liz was in the middle—swaying slightly. My new friend, Dick, and I were riding shotgun. We each had one arm around her waist—holding her up, moving her along. Squeezing her. Was this real? Did I really have my arm around Elizabeth Taylor's waist? Elizabeth Taylor—the movie idol, the most beautiful woman in the world. The star of *Cleopatra* (with my buddy Richard Burton as Marc Antony): *The Giant, A Place in the Sun, Cat on a Hot Tin Roof, Who's Afraid of Virginia Woolf,* and my favorite (an early one) *National Velvet,* made when Liz was just a kid. I was beginning to hyperventilate.

Finally we came to the entrance to my villa and paused. The three of us swayed back and forth. It was put-up or shut-up time. Would they invite me up to their place for a nightcap I wondered? No, but it was time to say goodnight and goodbye.

Liz leaned over and kissed me, first on one cheek, then on the other. It was a sweet moment. But I was holding out for more, for a full-on smooch on the lips. But it never arrived.

CHAPTER FORTY

ROCK 'N' ROLL AND THE ART OF FLY FISHING

I'm convinced that if I were a really good fly fisherman I wouldn't have so much fun fly fishing. Sounds strange I suppose, but let me tell you why. Fly fishing has enriched my life. It's also given me a quirky sense of the absurd. Sure, I like it when big Rainbows and Browns take notice of my fly's dead drift—at least I hope I'm dead-drifting it—but the act of fly fishing has become a platform for all the rest of it. The rest of it being a chance to drink some beer with my buddies, listen to rock 'n' roll and practice the art of snickering at Jeff, my fishing partner—and son by the way—and lacing into our guide-buddy Vince for his many transgressions.

I also like sitting in the drift boat, not fishing, just gazing out at the Tobacco Roots, the Absarokas, and once in a while spotting some nesting bald eagles.

That's all part of it. If I were a really good fly fisherman, I'm afraid I might be so absorbed with the act of fishing that I might lose all the other good stuff.

• • •

I was an absentee father. When Jeff was growing up he lived with his mother, and he and I weren't particularly close. He was a little stand-offish and I guess I was trying too hard to be his buddy. We are buddies now, even though he lives in Seattle and I live in San Francisco. It took years for us to establish a close friendship. One of the things that brought us together was fly fishing. Isn't it amazing how smart your kid gets the older he gets? Of course, Jeff says the same about me.

Sometimes back home here in San Francisco, leading the life I live— call it laid back—I wake up at night and think about fishing with Jeff and Vince. I have so much fun thinking about these fishing trips that I don't even care if I'm awake at three in the morning. Not only do I think about Jeff and Vince, but I mentally practice my casts and my cross body strikes.

. . .

Today we're fishing Montana's Lower Madison. The day is warm with a bit of cloud cover. I'm in the front on Vince's drift boat. Jeff brings up the rear. The boat is almost dead center in the river. I cast to a seam left front. Jeff casts right, toward the bank where some Canada Geese are raising a racket. I have on my line a dark Wooly Bugger with a tiny bead-head as a dropper. Jeff is fishing with a brown Wooly Bugger and a Red Worm.

. . .

"You missed him. He got away with something again," says Vince.

"What do you mean I missed him? What did I miss?" That's me talking.

"Yeah he did. He got away with it."

"No he didn't."

"Check your fly."

"Damn," I say. My bead is gone.

"Get back in the river. This looks fishy."

. . .

"Jeff's on," Vince says.

"Way to go Jeff." That's me again.

Jeff says nothing. He's busy.

. . .

"Jeff's on—again. Looks like Jeff's going to be pretty much hooked up all day."

"Way go Jeff, damn it." You know who said that.

Finally I get a good strike but I miss the fish. I'm daydreaming, not focused. Anyway, I burst into a song by the Who. Wagnerian rock, I call it.

I sing—*I won't get fooled again*—from the song of the same name.

Vince Gordon in his element. PHOTO: JEFF BEYL

"Yes, you will. You'll get skunked," says Vince.
Jeff keeps quiet. Then he's on another fine rainbow.
"Yeah, looks like Jeff's goin' to be pretty much hooked up all day."

• • •

Soon I get another strike. This time I manage to set the hook and the fish is off and running. I burst into song again. Same song but this time I sing the line this way — *I won't get skunked again.*

• • •

When it's time for lunch Vince swings the boat up onto a sandbar. We sit in the shade of a few stunted Cottonwoods on camp stools he keeps in the boat and tuck into some cold fried chicken, ripe tomatoes, oatmeal cookies, some cherries, and wash that down with root beer.

After lunch Jeff moves off and looks for interesting rocks washed by ancient glaciers. This is his normal, after lunch routine. He returns with a piece of tan shale and sits down cross-legged. He begins striking the shale with a stone he's picked up. A shard chips off. It looks like a crude spear point.

"Looks like a Clovis point," says Vince, and we are off discussing Clovis Man and how he may have come to North America on floating pack-ice from Europe where, archeologists say, the Clovis point technique originated. Did he come across the Atlantic or the long way around through Asia and over the Bering Strait, we wonder? Heavy duty!

• • •

Vince chips his own arrowheads. He gathers Red Dogwood shoots along the edges of the Yellowstone and Madison rivers. He peels off the bark and dries them for months and straightens them. Then he ties his arrowheads to the Dogwood shafts with strips of sinew and attaches feathers from wild turkeys that he shoots with his shotgun. Last year he got a turkey, kept some of the primary feathers for his arrow shafts and a friend made sausage with the turkey meat. Then Vince went out, and with one of his own arrows, shot a white tailed buck, skinned it out and filled his freezer with the meat. Now he wants to go all the way and make his own bow too. Vince tells us this on the sandbar over lunch. That was how Jeff started chipping arrowheads, straightening Dogwood shafts and reading books on primitive technology. I get my kicks trying to write these convoluted rock 'n' roll-fly fishing essays.

• • •

Late afternoon back on the river Jeff hooks up and in a minute later I do too. A double. Jeff's fish hits his Girtle Bug. I have on a Royal Wulff Parachute as an indicator and a Caddis Emerger as a dropper. My fish ignores the Parachute and goes for the dropper. We both burst into song. The Dylan tune—*Don't Think Twice It's All Right*. We sing in scratchy, nasal voices, emulating the young Dylan.

Vince slumps with laughter and releases the anchor so he can net and release our fish one after the other.

That's the way it goes on the lower Madison that day. I manage to get a few fairly decent Rainbows and one big Brown.

• • •

When we come off the river Vince's Bronco is there waiting for us. The shuttle driver has done her work. We pile in and listen to *Proud Mary* by Creedence and head for Land of Magic, the steakhouse in Logan, for some of those big, juicy rib-eyes, a baked potato, iceberg lettuce salad with ranch dressing out of the jar, and a bottle of red. I give Land of Magic my top rating.

Somehow rock—classic rock since we are of the classic rock age group—and fly fishing are compatible. They go together like those rib-eye steaks and baked potatoes with sour cream and chives. I can believe there are some fisher types who think fly fishing and Mozart might go together. As a matter of fact, they might work at that. That is, if Jeff and I could play air string quartet and cast at the same time.

• • •

The next day we fish DePuy Spring Creek in Paradise Valley near Livingston. The morning is bright and calm; only a slight breeze ruffles the pond in front of the DePuy anti-bellum, Gone-with-the-Wind mansion. That's right, mansion. An early DePuy apparently loved the movie and built the big white mansion which looks about two-thirds scale to the one they called Tara in the movie. The DePuy mansion sits incongruously at the edge of a spring-fed pond with the snow-topped Absarokas as a real—not movie fake—backdrop.

We put Vince's boat in the pond and float around. We are a good looking bunch of anglers if you don't pay attention to the hot sporting fashions of the day. Jeff's got a blue bandana tied around his head like Peter Fonda in *Easy Rider*. Vince wears his signature, beat-up wide brimmed straw hat. I wear my old baseball cap—brim forward I might add. Since it's already warm today we've stripped down to our t-shirts. Jeff's t-shirt reads Kerouac.com. Mine identifies itself as being from the Washington Square Bar & Grill, from my San Francisco neighborhood. Vince's t-shirt has no slogan and promotes nothing except Vince's stocky shoulders and chest. Vince needs no advertising validation. He constitutes an advertisement for himself.

While drifting silently around the pond and casting and retrieving dark green Wooly Buggers with Red Worms as droppers, we talk softly about how barometric pressure affects the fish and their dining habits.

Vince shows us how to do what he calls the Paula Maneuver. He had a client—a pretty good lady angler named Paula. After she let her nymph sink and just when she was about to get bored, retrieved it and cast again; she raised her rod tip slightly—just slightly. The nymph moved accordingly and more times than not, that was when she got a strike.

We try the Paula Maneuver and in a short while we hook into some good Rainbows and Browns.

Now we exchange ideas on something the three of us have decided to call Dynamic Convergence, a theory we have developed that when water temperature and air temperature are the same, or almost the same, fish strike eagerly. We think the theory works—just like the Paula Maneuver. It's that kind of day.

That afternoon we decide to fish the spring creek. We hike up-creek from the pond and Vince stakes Jeff out in a broad, riffled section and tells him to fish a black leech streamer.

"You're going to get some big ones," he says. "I'm going to take Ernie up to a good left-handed hole (I'm left handed) and see if I can keep him out of trouble. He won't get anything but he won't get into trouble either."

Sure enough, Vince leads me to a fine piece of water, with a confused current caused by some barely submerged rocks. Vince and I stand on the grassy right hand bank facing upstream. I have a small, orange foam indicator with a Girtle Bug and a Red Worm dropper. I cast, left-handed of course, upstream center just as Vince says I should. Fine for a moment but then the indicator plunges right over the large, slightly submerged rock that's dead center and the rig jerks downstream in a hustling hurry. That doesn't work.

When I get the proper drift, this side or the other side of the rock things go better. In a few minutes I have hooked a few 15- to 18-inch Rainbows.

Out of the corner of my eye I see Jeff approaching on the other side of the creek.

"Bad news," Vince predicts—and it is.

"Nothing," Jeff says simply.

"Not even one strike?" I say.

"Not one."

From the other side of the creek Jeff stands watching me. Another fish takes my Red Worm, I play him for a minute or two and Vince makes his way downstream to the edge of the water and releases the fish carefully. In the next 15 minutes the scene is repeated three times. Jeff watches me. He's not having a good afternoon. With a great show of phony fellowship, I hand my rod over to Jeff.

"Go get a fish," I say.

Ruefully, he agrees and takes up my post streamside. Vince and I find a couple of good rocks nearby to sit on and prepare for our heckling dialogue. Because he is right-handed, Jeff begins to cast backhanded.

"Just this side of the rock," instructs Vince.

Then, in rapid sequence:

"Just the other side of the rock."

"Not on the rock dipshit, one side or the other."

I snicker audibly.

Then on the same cast, Vince instructs "Mend up." (Pause) "Mend down." (Pause) "Don't mend."

Then just before Jeff's next cast: "Right reach." "Choke."

Then, "Mend up." (Pause) "Mend down." (Pause) "Don't mend."

I snicker.

A bit later, Jeff snags the dropper on the big rock and loses the entire rig. With mock patience, Vince rigs the line again. I continue to snicker.

"Lay it out for god's sake."

Silent up to now—except for the loud snickering—I take my shot: "At least you had a good morning at the pond."

"Screw the pond," Jeff replies.

A wind has come up. Heavy clouds advance from upstream. A few big drops dot the water.

"Here it comes. We're outta here," yells Vince.

"Five more casts," Jeff says.

Well, you can anticipate this I suppose. On the last cast Jeff hooks up.

It's a good Rainbow. He looks over his shoulder at Vince and me and gives us a shallow smile.

Vince releases Jeff's fish and we dash for the Bronco as the thunder cracks. We pile in and open three cold beers from the cooler. Vince clicks on the radio and searches for a particular Clapton cut on a CD Jeff made for him. It's *Stormy Monday*, the T-Bone Walker classic.

They call it stormy Monday; (today happens to be Monday) *but Tuesday's just as bad.*
Wednesday's even worse, Thursday's awful sad.
The eagle flies on Friday, Saturday I go out to play.
Sunday, I go to church where I kneel down and pray.

It's positively Mozartian in its thrust. Clapton (who happens to be a fly fisherman) kicks ass—his guitar wickedly bending the blue notes, his thin voice relating the story.

As we drive along back to Bozeman in the now receding storm, we feel good. We listen to a little traveling music—*Jessica* by the Allman Brothers, Stevie Ray Vaughan's *It's Flooding Down in Texas,* and Dylan's *Mr. Tambourine Man.* As a coda to the day, Jeff and I once more burst into song:

Hey! Mr. Tambourine man, play a song for me,
I'm not sleepy and there is no place I'm going to.
Hey! Mr. Tambourine man, play a song for me,
In the jingle jangle morning I'll come followin' you.
Then take me disappearin' through the smoke rings of my mind,
Da, da, da, da, da, da, da
Da, da, da, da, da, da, da
Da, da, da, da, da….
Let me forget about today until tomorrow."

ACKNOWLEDGMENTS:
SOURCES AND INSPIRATIONS

It has taken me a long time to write this book—almost a lifetime. Throughout many years as a traveler I have always made notes. And frequently I've adorned my travel notebooks with small, crude sketches to later jog my memory about where I've been and what I've experienced.

I have wanted to write a travel book for just about as long as I can remember. It was really the U.S. Marine Corps that gave me my travel chops. World War II was over in 1945. I joined the Marine Corps in 1946 and after boot camp in San Diego (I suppose that was a travel adventure in itself), I was put on a troop ship, sailed under San Francisco's Golden Gate Bridge, and headed out into the Pacific Ocean. I'll avoid inflicting you with further biographical references here. Elsewhere in this book there's a section called *About the Author* so if you're inclined you can dip into it.

When I was in the Marine Corps I read everything I could get my hands on. This included a lot of travel books. They nurtured my desire to adopt a traveler's life. I still read travel books today. Some of these I have written about in the introduction to this book. Others, listed below, are some I found enlightening and useful. I have also included in this list some books I needed in my research.

Borrowed Place Borrowed Time by Richard Hughes (Andre Deutsch 1968)

Etchings in an Hourglass by Kate Simon (Harper Perennial 1990)

The Great Railway Bazaar by Paul Theroux (Houghton Mifflin Company 1975)

The House on the Klong by William Warren (Privately printed, Tokyo 1968)

In Patagonia by Bruce Chatwin (Jonathan Cape Ltd. 1977)

Island of Bali by Miguel Covarrubias (Alfred A. Knopf 1956)

Jim Thompson the Legendary American of Thailand by William Warren

(Asia Books Co., Ltd. 1976)

The Pillars of Hercules by Paul Theroux (Fawcett Books 1995)

Riding the Red Rooster by Paul Theroux (G.P Putnam Sons 1988)

The River at the Center of the World by Simon Winchester (Henry Holt and Company 1996)

The Scents of Eden by Charles Corn (Kodansha International 1998)

Ships & How They Sailed the Seven Seas by Hendrik Willem van Loon (Simon and Shuster 1935)

The Songlines by Bruce Chatwin (Viking Penguin Inc. 1987)

To Get Rich is Glorious by Orville Schell (Pantheon Books 1984)

And now, here are a few people who have been instrumental in my writing of *Stops along the Royal Road:*

Joan Beyl, Laurel Beyl, and Jeff Beyl—I must cluster these three members of my immediate family. I wouldn't know how to rank them vertically in proper order. All three have shared many travel adventures with me. You will find them in the pages of this book. Additionally, my wife Joan is my best and most sensitive editor. She not only encourages me in my writing, but frequently pulls me back from the abyss of overwriting. My daughter Laurel has a great ear. When I read my work aloud to her a thumbs-up or thumbs-down sets me straight. My son Jeff, also a writer (and a fine one) is my fishing buddy. He's like a younger brother to me.

Paul Theroux—This extraordinary novelist and travel writer has been a major influence on me. When I read his first travel book, *The Great Railway Bazaar*, I was astonished. It inspired me, as have other books he has written. Theroux is a true wanderer—curious, exacting, and at times, a bit cantankerous.

Daniel David—My Grizzly Peak Press publisher, Daniel David, gave me a chance. He accepted my first book for publication, then my second, and now my third. What a guy!

Sara Brownell—My gal-pal Sara Brownell designs my books. She is incredibly talented and I am indebted to her for making my work look so good.

Fred Lyon—I have an unbounded admiration for photographer Fred Lyon and the work he has done over the many years he has been my friend. Fortunately, Fred and I have been able to travel together on many assignments.

Lawrence Ferlinghetti—I count this poet, painter, pamphleteer, and publisher as a friend. I hope some of his magic has rubbed off on me.

Herbert Gold—This master novelist and travel writer has always encouraged me to write what I know personally and what I have experienced. I have tried to do just that in this book. If I have succeeded, he has succeeded in mentoring me.

Arthur Adams—Photographer Arthur Adams died several years ago. I remember him with pleasure since he was part of many of my travel adventures. Arthur was a wonderful traveling companion.

Portions of this book have appeared previously in a variety of publications. These include—*San Valley Magazine, Big Sky Journal, The Marina Times, Northside San Francisco, POSH, The Seabourn Club Herald,* and *California Fly Fisher.*

Ernest Beyl
San Francisco, March 2018

ABOUT THE AUTHOR

Ernest Beyl is a San Francisco author whose insatiable desire for travel has been an overpowering urge since he was a youngster. He counts himself fortunate he has been able to realize his ambition. *Stops along the Royal Road* is his newest book. To date he has written three—*Sketches from a North Beach Journal, San Francisco Appetites and Afterthoughts*, and this new book that recounts his lifetime of travel adventures.

As a kid the he was fascinated by Richard Halliburton, a romantic loner who spent his life traveling on what he called *The Royal Road to Romance*—hence the reference in the title of this book. Our author says, "I first read Halliburton when I was in knee pants. The man had an uncontrollable itch to move around the globe. I have that itch as well."

Wanting to follow Halliburton's footsteps, at 18 Ernest Beyl joined the U.S. Marine Corps which seemed to him the most practical way to do it. Following peacetime service in Southeast Asia and the Pacific he attended Stanford University. Following graduation he became a copyboy, then a reporter for the *San Francisco Chronicle*. A stint as a Hollywood press agent and PR executive convinced him to get back to the Royal Road.

Today he spends his time working on book projects, and writing freelance articles about his favorite city, San Francisco, its history and its culture. He is married to Joan Lawson Beyl, has a son and a daughter, and lives on San Francisco's Telegraph Hill.

INDEX

A Field Guide to Western Birds, 105

A Place in the Sun, 141

A Year in Provence, 117

Adams, Arthur, 57-59, 153

Adams, Nick, 92, 100

Alexandra, H.R.H., Princess, 48

Alexandria Quartet, The, 117

Allman Brothers, 150

Alsace-Lorraine, 53

Angel Falls, 89-91

Angel, Jimmie, 90-91

Arabian Nights, The, 36

Asiatics, The, xvii-xix

Au Boon Haw, 125

Bacall, Lauren, 110, 111

Bali, 58, 60-62, 130

Ball, Lucille, 94

Balthazar, 115, 117

Bangkok, 57, 68, 129

Bardot, Brigette, 117

Beijing, 17-19, 36-37

Bencharong, 130

Berle, Milton, 95

Berners, Dame Juliana, 92

Beyl, Jeff, 103-105, 124-127, 143-150

Bieger, Felix, 49-52

Big Two-Hearted River, 92

Bingham, Hiram, 42

Blue Damsels, 103-105

Bogart, Humphrey, 111

Book of the Thousand Nights and
    a Night, 36

Borrowed Place, Borrowed Time, 52

Botafumeiro, 136-137

Bouillabaisse, 116-117

Boyer Les Crayeres, 121-122

Boyer, Gerard, 121

Bozzi, Pio, 119

Brasserie Lipp, 120

Brooke, James, 36

Brown Derby, The, 111, 113-114

Brynner, Yul, 69

Bugis Street, 106

Bung Sukarno, 57-59

Burckhardt, Jacob, 117

Burton, Richard, 79, 111, 139-141

Burton, Sir Richard Francis, 36

Byron, Lord, 115

CAAC, 17

Cagnes sur Mer, 122

Capote, Truman, 116

Cat on a Hot Tin Roof, 141

Cathay Pacific Airways, xx, vi, 45, 63, 78-79

Chan, Sau-king, 124-127

Chandler, Raymond, 120

Chasen's, 111-112

Chatwin, Bruce, xvii, 151-152

Chen, Clement, 17

Childe Harold's Pilgrimage, 115

Chili Crab, 107-108

Churchill, Winston, 117

Civilization of the Renaissance, 117

Clapton, 115

Clapton, Eric, 115

Claudius, 117

Clea, 117

Cleopatra, 111, 117, 141

Cobb Salad, 113-114

Cockpit, The, 57-58

Colbert, Claudette, 94

Collier's Magazine, 119

Colossus of Maroussi, The, 118

Columbus, Christopher, 37

Comedians, The, xx

Compleat Angler, The, 6, 92

Confucius, 131

Conrad, Joseph, xvii

Cook, Thomas, 36

Cooper, Gary, 94, 100-102

Cooper, Rocky, 101-102

Cordoba, Jesus, 86-88

Covarrubias, Miguel, 60, 151

Creedence Clearwater Revival, 104, 147

Creedence, 104, 147

Cuzco, 25, 38-42

Dali, Salvador, 79, 116

Death in the Afternoon, 88

Death in Venice, 117

Deep South, xx

Delaplane, Stanton, xvii

Denpasar, 58

DePuy Spring Creek, 147

Dirty Harry, 16

Don Francisco Pizarro, 23, 24

Don't Think Twice It's All Right, 146

Dorsey, Tommy, 16

Douglas, Kirk, 111-112

Dozier's Barbecue, 77-78

Dragon Air, 15

Duffill, xx-xxi

Duffill, R., xx-xxi

Durgin Park, 80

Durrell, Lawrence, 115, 117

Dutch East India Company, 21

Dylan, Bob, v, xiv, 104, 146, 150

Easy Rider, 147

Eddy Duchin Lounge, 101

Eileen, Yin-fei Lo, 131-133

Emperor Hirohito, 32-34

Emperor Zhu Houcong, 17-19

Evil Eye beads, 130

Fassett, Bill and Lolly, 79

Faulkner, William, 120

Ferretti, Fred, 20

Fior D'Italia, 121

Fitzgerald, F. Scott, 120

Floria, Johnny, 57

Flynn, Erroll, 94

Fonda, Peter, 147

Food Paper, The, 108

Food of France, The, 53

For Whom the Bell Tolls, 95-97, 101

Forbidden City, 17-19

Fortnum and Mason, 130

Frank Lloyd Wright, 28

Frousy Fanny, 1-7

Gable, Clark, 94, 113

Ganzi, John, 119

Ganzi, Wally, 119

Gardner, Ava, 140

Garuda, 58

Gellhorn, Martha, 95

Gerguson, Harry, 11

Giant, The, 141

Goddard, Paulette, 94

Godwin Park Hotel, 21

Gordon, General Charles George
    "Chinese", 36

Gordon, Mack, 94

Gordon, Vince, xiii, xv, 82, 143-150

Grand Bazaar of Istanbul, 130

Gravlax, 113

Great Railway Bazaar, The, xx-xxi, 151-152

Great Wall of China, The, 18

Greene, Graham, xvii, xix-xx

Greenstreet, Sydney, 75

Gringo Gulch, 138-142

Hadrian, 117

Halliburton, Richard, xvii-xviii, 155

Hammerstein, Oscar, 68

Han Dynasty, 128

Hannagan, Steve, 94-96, 101, 113, 120

Hansen, Ken, 113
Harilela, 44, 50-51
Harilela, Peter N., 50
Harriman, W. Averill, 94
Harry's Café de Wheels, 81
Hav, xxii
Hayworth, Rita, 79
Heart of the Matter, The, xx
Hemingway, Ernest, xvii, xiv, 86-88, 92-102,
    104-105, 130
Hemingway, Mary, 100-102
Henie, Sonja, 95
Himalaya, 74-76
Hirohito, 32-34
Hitchcock, Alfred, 111-112
Holiday Inn, 17
Hong Kong and Shanghai Hotels, Ltd.,
    46, 63
Hong Kong Arts Festival, 48-50
Hong Kong Foreign Correspondent's Club,
    52, 125
Hong Kong, 43-52, 124-127
Huangpu, The, 8-10, 15
Huayna Picchu, 38, 42
Hughes, Richard, 52, 151
Huston, John, 140
Imperial Hotel, 28, 31
Imperial Palace, 19, 32-34
In Our Time, 92, 100, 104
Incas, 23,-24, 26, 38-42
Island of Bali, 58, 60-62, 151
It Happened in Sun Valley, 94-95
It's Flooding Down in Texas, 150
Italy, the Places Between, 117
Jakarta, 21, 57-58
James, Henry, xvii
Jeff, 103-105, 124-127, 143-150
Jiajing Emperor, 17-19
Jianguo Hotel, 17
Josy-Jo, 122-123
Journey without Maps, xx

Justine, 117
Kadoorie, Lord Lawrence, 46-47, 128
Kadoorie, Sir Horace, 46-47
Kenton, Stan, 120
Kerouac, Jack, 79
Kerr, Deborah, 69
Ketchum, 97, 101, 103-105
King and I, The, 68-69, 129
Kowloon, 43, 46, 50, 63, 70
Kuala Lumpur, 57
Landor, Walter, 138-139
Lava, Lava, 75-76
Lawrence, Gertrude, 69
Lei Yue Mun, 63-67
Les Crayeres, 121-122
Lewis, John, 122-123
Lewis, Norman, xx
Little Rivers, 92
Lobby of the Pen, 44, 49, 64, 67, 72
Lombard, Carole, 113-114
Lorca Museum, 25-27
Lorca Pre-Columbian Museum, 25
Lord Kadoorie, 128
Loren, Sophia, 111
Louvre, 130
Luk Yu Tea House, 119
M.F.K. Fisher, 118
MacArthur, 28-31, 33
MacArthur, General Douglas, 28-31, 33
Machu Picchu, xiv, 24, 25, 38, 41, 42
MacLehose, His Excellency, the Governor,
    48-50
Madison River, xiii
Mahesh Mararishi, 79
Mandarin Oriental, The, 45
Mann, Thomas, 117
Mansfield, Jayne, 111
Mao Zedong, 46, 131
Mapo Doufu, 37
Marco Polo, xxii, 21, 35
Marx, Groucho, 110, 113

Maugham, W. Somerset, xvii-xviii
Mayle, Peter, 117
Miller, Glenn, 15, 94-95
Miller, Henry, 79, 118
Ming Tombs, 17-19
Mismaloya, 140
Mister Emmrich, 1-7
Modern Jazz Quartet, xiv, 122
Modigliani, 122
Mongkok, 70-72, 125
Morris, Jan, xvii, xxii
Mosquito Coast, The, xx
Mountolive, 117
Moveable Feast, 120
Mr. Tambourine Man, 150
Mrs. Pockmark's Bean Curd, 37
Musso and Frank's Grill, 120
Musso and Frank's, 110, 114, 120
Musso, Joseph, 120
My Secret History, xx
National Geographic Society, 42
National Geographic, 38
National Velvet, 141
Nehru, Prime Minister Jawaharal, 62
Nepenthe, 79-80
Nero, 117
New Worlds to Conquer, xviii
Night of the Iguana, The, 140
Nonya cuisine, xiv, 107-109
Nonya, 107-109
Obernai, 53
Oblensky-Romanoff, Prince Michael
    Dimitri Alexandrovich, 111
Oceano Hotel, 138-140
Odyssey, The, 115
Old Clam House, The, 121
Old Man and the Sea, The, 97
Old Patagonian Express, The, xx
Oon, Violet, 107-109
Ordonez, Antonio, xiv, 85-91
Ordonez, Cayetano, 85

Orinoco River, 89
P&O, 73-76
P&O-Orient Lines, 43, 73-76
P.O.S.H., 74
Palm Too, 119
Palm, The, 119
Payne, John, 95
Peck, Gregory, 112
Pen, The, 49, 125
Peninsula Group, 17
Peninsula Hotel, 17, 44-49, 64, 72, 124, 128
Peninsular and Oriental Steam Navigation
    Company, 73
People's Republic of China, 45, 51, 70
Peranakan cuisine, 107-109
Peranakan, 107-109
Perino's, 111-113
Peterson, Roger Tory, 104
Pfeiffer, Pauline, 95
Pillars of Hercules, The, xx, 117, 152
Pommery Metropole, 121
Porno Pottery, 25-27
Porto Ordaz, 89
Posh, 73, 153
President Xi Jinping, 19
Prince Romanoff, 111
Prokosch, Frederic, xvii-xx
Proud Mary, 147
Quiet American, The, xx
Rajah, Brooke, 36
Reagan, Ronald, 111
Reception Café, 121
Regent, The, 45
Renoir, Pierre-Augustus, 122
Riding the Red Rooster, xx, 152
Rijsttafel, 20-22, 56
Roads, David, 50-52
Rodgers, Richard, 68
Romanoff's, 111
Root, Waverley, 53
Ross, Harold, 111

Royal Road to Romance, The, xvii, 155
Sacsayhuaman, 40
Sam's Grill and Seafood Restaurant, 120-121
Sam's Grill, vii, 120-121
Scandia, 111, 113
Schroeder's, 121
Shanghai, 8-14, 15-16, 46
Shearer, Norma, 94
Sheridan, Ann, 120
Silver Creek, 98-99, 101-102, 103-105
Simon, Kate, xvii, 117, 151
Sinatra, Frank, 111-112
Sinclair, Kevin, 52
Singapore Airlines, 64
Singapore, 21, 36, 57, 83-84, 106, 107-108
Sir Scott's Oasis, 81-82
Stanislaus River, 2, 5-6
Stevenson, Robert Louis, xvii
Stewart, Jimmy, 111
Stormy Monday, 150
Strasbourg, vi, 53
Suetonius, 117
Suetonius's Lives of the Twelve Caesars, 117
Sukarno, 57-59
Sukarno, Achmed, 57-59
Sultan of Brunei, The, 36
Summer Palace, 17
Sun Also Rises, The, 93, 100, 104
Sun Valley Serenade, 94
Sun Valley, 92, 94-97, 98, 101, 103, 104
Suyin, Han, 52
Symonds, John Addington, 116
Tadich Grill, 120
Taix, 110
Taylor, Elizabeth, 79, 138-142
Ted Bear, 45, 52
Temple of Heaven, 17, 18
Thai silk, 68-69, 129
Theroux, Paul, xvii, xx-xxi, 117, 151-152
Thompson, Jim, 68-69, 129, 151

Thorey Lyautey, 55-56
thurible, 137
Tiananmen Square, 18
Tiberius, 117
Tiger Balm Gardens, 125
Tiraboleiros, 137
Tommy's, 110
Toulet, Frank, 120
Tracy, Spencer, 111
Treatise of Fishing with an Angle, 92
Trillin, Calvin, 83
Tupac, Amaru, 42
Turner, Joseph M.A., 116
Turner, Lana, 111
Two Towns in Provence, 118
U.S. Marine Corps, 8, 151, 155
Ubud, 61, 130
Union Pacific Railroad, 94
Urubamba River, 25
Valley of the Ming Tombs, 17-19
Van Dyke, Henry, 92
Van Guilder, Gene, 95
Vaughan, Stevie Ray, 104, 150
Voices, A Memoir, xix
Walker, T-Bone, 150
Walton, Izaak, 6, 92
Warren, Harry, 94
Washington Square Bar & Grill, 119, 147
Wayne, John, 113
Welles, Orson, 79
Westphal, Scott, 82
White Rajahs of Sarawak, 36
Who, The, 144
Who's Afraid of Virginia Woolf, 141
William Fellers, Colonel, 28
Williams, Taylor "Beartracks", 96-97, 101, 104-105
Yangtze River, 8-9
Yellowstone River, xiii, 104
Zenovich, Sam, 121
Zhu Houcong, 17-19